Nice Guys Finish First

D0879696

Doug Sandler

Published by Motivational Press, Inc.
1777 Aurora Road
Melbourne, Florida, 32935
www.MotivationalPress.com

Manufactured in the United States of America.

ISBN: 978-1-62865-161-4

CONTENTS

DEDICATION

Danielle, thank you for believing in me, especially during those brief times when I didn't believe in myself. Your encouragement, advice, cheerleading and example make me feel like I can accomplish anything.

Mom, you have always supported me, and for that, I am so very grateful.

Adam and Rachel, you are the world to me and I am so proud of all you do. I am so lucky to have you as my children.

wd - I love you, +1 - BD

ACKNOWLEDGEMENTS

Special thanks to Rob Jolles for keeping me on the path to write this book. Thank you to Jane Atkinson for helping me pick a lane and Ryan Estis for teaching me to burn the boats and for being a great role model. Thank you Michael Steinhardt for telling me to get busy, without delay. Justin Sachs, thank you for believing in my book and letting me sound my voice.

Thanks also goes to Robert Sherman, Chuck Kahanov, Jack Hartzman, Strickland Bonner, Carroll Higgins and Angel Santiago for being great business partners and giving me time to feed my new life and encourage me to follow my dreams.

Special thanks to my friends Scott Miller, Bruce Shapiro, David Sax, Mike Skirven, Ken Cosco, Fern Sandler, Aaron Gold, Mike Gordon, Fresh and Glyde.

To my Uncle Morris (1931-2015), a legend in life and beyond, thank you for being a trusted advisor.

Mom, Marty, Nancy, Richard, David, Adam, Rachel, I love you very much and appreciate your support

PREFACE

The concept of being a nice guy has always been with me. I can remember being a kid and my mom saying to me, as I was about to go to school, "Dougie, be nice." As if being nice was going to get me places, help me achieve success and make all of my dreams come true. Little did I know. How could I know? I was just a kid.

Nice equates to enjoyable, pleasant, good and delightful. But I don't recall anyone ever saying that if I was nice I would be a winner, and with nice as a part of my behavior, I would absolutely be happier. It wasn't until many years later as a novice salesman did I realize that you could get a lot more out of people if you were nice to them.

Conversely, being not nice, if you lived in my childhood home, would be grounds for punishment. And since I was respectful, and the baby of my family, I was the nicest kid in town. I truly believe that it was my mother's personal conviction that you should always leave someone feeling better about themselves than before you met with them. And she did just that. My mom has been a real estate agent since the mid-1970s. In my hometown, you can't go into a coffee shop or a local store without running into at least one person she has sold a house to. Even now in her early 80s, she still goes to the office, writes a contract every now and then and is genuinely loved by everyone that knows her. Technology has really set her back though, and soon I feel she will be hanging up her license and hitting the cruise circuit with my step-dad, Marty. The two of them love a good buffet.

Growing up I had a fairly normal childhood. My parents divorced when I was only 2 years old, and a few years later my mom remarried. I think in today's social climate in America, that's pretty normal. My brother, David, who is 4 years older, always seemed to be one step ahead of me. Wherever I was going, he had been there just a few years before. Funny thing though, we could not be more opposite from one another. My teachers and community leaders were in for a big surprise as little Dougie entered into his big brother's shadow. David excelled at team sports, and while I was athletic, I could care less about sports. As a radio and television major, David went on to become our town celebrity, doing traffic on the most popular radio stations in our market. His success in radio has been wonderful, and I have always been so proud of his accomplishments. Despite our differences, we almost never fought, and I enjoy the relationship we now share.

It wasn't until I graduated college and entered the workforce that I turned from a nice guy to a nice guy finishing first. It seemed that the lessons I learned as a little kid were paying off. My default was to be nice because the voice in my head was my mom's saying, "Dougie, be nice." Thanks to her advice, I have learned that people respond positively to nice guys.

Out of college and in the real world I focused on making money. If it was legal, moral and ethical, and I could make money doing it, I wanted in. I was a capitalist on a mission. And while the fundamental idea of being nice stayed with me, I would listen to cassette tapes, read books on success and attend free seminars on the subject of building a successful career. At the time, being nice was just an add-on. No matter how much money I was making, it wasn't enough. I was lacking balance, and for many years I was searching for opportunity after opportunity. Early on in my career I changed jobs often, because I always thought I could make more and have a higher level position at the next one. For me, it was all about the title and the money. It wasn't until I had a job in the mortgage business that I realized there is more to life than just money. Money was not the means to happiness. I took mortgage applications for very wealthy people, and I discovered they were not any happier than me. My boss Brian would always say, "Doug, we are all broke, just at different levels. The guy making $100,000 has a $3,500 mortgage payment and drives a car with a $1,500 payment." He was right. My mom also had a saying. "Money can't buy happiness, but it helps you arrive at your problems in style." I was living a life of paying bills, driving my Mercedes and arriving at my problems in style.

We spend very little time in school or on the job learning about how to be happy. I call it the "happy factor." Billions of dollars are spent on buying self-improvement books yet the vast majority of time we spend in school and at job training is spent on practical knowledge. That is, the application of what we are learning and how it applies in the field we are learning about.

But what about the positive effects of being happy? Happy is an incredibly powerful state of mind. Happiness is not created from material wealth. It is not created by external influences at all. So what is it that causes us to be happy? Over the years and through a huge level of experience I have learned that happiness is completely up to each and every one of us. Your being happy is up to you and no one else.

The biggest factor that creates happiness is positive self-talk. We all have ways of building ourselves up. Conversely, we often use self-talk to tear ourselves down. Positive self-talk is extremely effective in helping produce a positive outcome. Just as negative self-talk will work against us and create a negative outcome.

Being your own worst critic is a big challenge to overcome. In this book, I will provide a roadmap that will guide you to understand why being nice is a gateway trait to being happy. You cannot build a house of success and wins on a foundation of negativity and discontent. As you are reading this book, you will understand that you can be successful at anything you attempt. There is no doubt you will have setbacks along the way. I can even guarantee it. Henry Ford said, "Whether you think you can or think you can't, you are right." Your role is to not give up. Never quit and never get out of the game.

I was making great money, I was a nice guy and I was finishing first. So why wasn't I happy? I set a goal in 1997 to find my happy place and I worked hard at finding myself. My love of music and my business knowledge and sales skills turned a part-time business of being a club-type DJ into a full-time mobile DJ career. I hired an agent in 1998 and have not looked back since. I've performed at over 2,000 functions in my career, and, as of the writing of this book, still perform at over 75 gigs annually in the high-end Washington, D.C. social market.

I love my work for two main reasons. First, I love my clients. I am celebrating a milestone with them, and they have entrusted me with that responsibility. Second, I get to party for a living, and as a guy who is constantly happy and nice (thanks to my mom) it has been an incredible career. The side benefit to loving my work in addition to being happy is that I am able to support my family as a result.

For well over 15 years and thousands of clients later, I have built a system that is time-tested. I believe that if you provide exceptional customer service, world class in style, and you believe in what you are doing and it makes you happy, then you will be successful. But it requires effort. My system is about investing time, energy and resources in inspiring my prospects and customers to take action and helping them make decisions and execute their plans in the most efficient way..

Follow my system, take note of the lessons I have learned and you will be headed down the path toward success and happiness.

Our world today is filled with companies who think of their customers as 16-digit numbers, and it's time to put the *service* back in customer service. It's time to be human and handle people like they are people. I promise you, especially with the technology we have today at our use, there is room for nice guys. There is plenty of room to be happy, successful and balanced. Take note, we—the happy, successful and balanced—are the exception to the rule, but I will show you beyond a shadow of a doubt that you too can build your business the way that I have built mine. Invest, inspire and execute, but above all be nice, and you will find out that the world needs more nice people. Nice guys finish first.

FOREWORD

"THE SHORTEST ANSWER IS DOING THE RIGHT THING"

Do nice guys really finish first? My friend Doug Sandler certainly seems to think so. Doug not only believes it; he lives it every day of his life. It's something that I have admired in him from the moment I met him. I just didn't know if I believed him.

When I first heard Doug talking about the concept of "nice people finishing first," I thought this to myself: "That's nice… good for you." It wasn't as if I had never heard this phrase before; I just had not heard the phrase since elementary school. Along with so many other wonderful, uncomplicated, innocent messages I learned when I was growing up, I stopped believing that nice guys finish first once I grew up and entered the working world.

It wasn't as if this concept was being reinforced in any professional manner. I don't remember hearing my high school teachers, nor my college professors ever telling me this. I don't remember taking any corporate training programs reinforcing this concept. As a matter of fact, if you Google the phrase, "nice guys finish first, the phrase that pops up is "nice guys finish last!" Somewhere along the way, the principle that nice people finish first was forgotten and the disciplines of this basic belief were lost.

Then Doug Sandler emerged. He plowed past the naysayers, and he did something that was far more difficult than just writing about this principle. He did something that was significantly more courageous; he decided to *live* this principle. Even more impressive, he has lived this principle for well over two decades, and he never expected anything in return.

While living by this principle, a funny thing happened. The more good things he did, the more he received in return. By going the extra mile, doing the right thing, and expecting nothing in return for the many things he gave away, he found a higher level of success then he had ever experienced before. He took control of the situation. By doing this, he found a higher level of happiness. That's one of the many gifts he is offering you within these pages.

You can decide to be a good person and you can decide to do the right thing; It's 100% under your control, and being in control makes people happier. Think back to a time when you felt happy. I'm going to guess that you may have also felt in control of your life. You were in control of your job, in control of your relationships, and you felt you had control of your health. Conversely, think back on times when you felt unhappy. I'll bet you might remember a lack of control about your circumstances at that time.

A fascinating study took place at Rutgers University, and it dealt with the relationship between control and happiness. The study used babies as the participants, and they found that, even for babies, there was a higher level of happiness for the test group that felt more in control! That's right, even babies felt happier when they felt in control!

Here's how they proved it. They created a test I'll refer to as "the String Test." In this test, a string was attached to different babies' wrists. It took a little while, but eventually, the babies figured out that by pulling the string, pictures would appear in front of them. I've seen a video of this and there was no question that those babies were thrilled! They learned that they had a wonderful source of amusement by just pulling the string. Then they disconnected the string, and although the babies continued to pull, it no longer showed any pictures. As a result, the babies weren't amused anymore and they began to withdraw, and some of them cried for a short period of time.

However, what made me sit up and take a deeper look at this test was what happened next. Pictures began to appear randomly, and although the babies continued to pull the string, it had no effect on when these pictures would appear. In short, control was taken from the babies. They were not only frustrated, but they were much more upset. There wasn't a baby in the bunch who didn't cry – loudly. When they were given the control back, they were happy again.

Case study after case study keeps telling us the same thing. In car manufacturing plants, management learned that the workers were unhappy and had low morale. How did they turn it around? They gave the assembly line workers the ability to stop the assembly line if there was an issue. Control.

Adapting the principles behind *Nice Guys Finish First* is under your control, and control makes us happy. When you think about it, adapting Doug Sandler's principles of doing the right thing in business and in life creates a win-win-win situation. It's a win for those you affect by practicing these principles. It's a win for the business you operate, and it's a win for you personally.

I'm quite sure you will not only be inspired by Doug Sandler's words, but you will also learn the easy and common sense approach he provides. After all, learning how and why *Nice Guys Finish First*, and applying it to so many elements outlined in business and life, sounds like a can't miss formula for the application of these principals in your world.

———

My concern is *will* you implement his words? You see, I happen to know Doug Sandler, and I know that he won't be happy with your just reading his book. Doug wants you to go beyond just being inspired and entertained by his book. He wants you to implement what he has written in your everyday activities.

I'm going to add my voice to his and ask the same thing: When you have finished reading this book, walk away with the commitment that you will make a cultural change in how you interact with others. If you do so, I can guarantee you two things: First, doing the right thing will *not* diminish your chances of success. Second, doing the right thing will make you, and those around you, happier and more successful.

I must admit that I had a little help with the title of this forward. Ernest Hemingway once said this: "The shortest answer is doing the thing." Speaking for Doug, I want to build on that quote and I want you to remember this: "The shortest answer is doing the *right* thing." The world is your oyster when you do! Enjoy this joyful and intelligently crafted book, written by a sensitive and caring man who lives by the principle: *Nice Guys Finish First.* He is living proof of how truthful his words truly are.

Rob Jolles

Author *How to Change Minds*

CHAPTER 1

WHY NICE GUYS FINISH FIRST

Nice guys finish first. If you don't know that, then you don't know where the finish line is.

~Gary Shandling

In 1992, I was a rock star. Eight years into a crazy career in social event entertainment, I was flying business class to New Orleans to work my dream job. A client, who I had never met, had never spoken to and knew nothing about, hired me sight unseen to work their celebration. You see, I was a wedding singer, except I was not a singer, but a DJ. And this wasn't a wedding, it was a bar mitzvah. Regardless, I was prepaid, full of ego, living large and loving life. I was treated to a hotel room and had all of my expenses covered. I had made the big time, or so I thought. It was about to get real very soon.

At a time when others in the industry were making $300 per event, I was making $2,000 at this gig (that's what rock stars call them, *gigs*). I had a driver pick me up at my hotel, drive me around the French Quarter and Bourbon Street. I stopped for a wonderful lunch, paid for by the client, at an authentic New Orleans restaurant. My driver delivered me to the venue for the event. The room was beautifully decorated with colorful balloons, beautiful linen, lights in all the right hues and tones, fragrant flowers, tapered candles and fun themed props.

But reality was about to hit me right between the eyes. In addition to 75 or so adults, the guest list included 50 plus young people. I would call them children, but that word brings thoughts of innocence, giggles and fun. I'll just call them what they were. Monsters! Within 15 minutes of this four hour event, they managed to dismantle the centerpieces on their tables, suck the helium out of every single balloon, ignite toilet paper on fire in the bathroom and throw pea soup on the walls and windows in the hallway. Only one sixteenth into this four hour event and it was already over. The party was out of control, spiraling down quickly in a plume of dark smoke and flames. Each progressive moment was getting worse. And guess who the host and hostess wanted to control this rampage? Me!

I did what I thought any self-respecting entertainer should do when faced with an out of control crowd and a battlefield. I retreated to the comfort zone of the stage and my turntables, put my head down, my headphones on and gave up. At that point, I really knew it was over. I had lost the battle. I'd never felt so low and defeated as I felt just then. I mean, how could these monsters do this to ME?

The rest was a blur. I do not recall checking out of the hotel or my flight back home. I can't seem to recall the call from my agent to talk about the horrible experience. There was no driver to collect me and whisk me away. There was no tour of historic districts and no royal treatment. They wanted me out. What I can remember, however, with absolutely clarity, was writing the refund check. Two grand is a lot of money, especially because I already spent it.

My discovery? Had I actually had a conversation with my client, prior to the event date, I would have discovered these "kids" had been to 49 other events that year and this was the final celebration.

Had I invested a bit of time and planned the event with my client, we would have come up with an alternate plan. But rock stars don't make phone calls to clients, because rock stars have huge egos and know everything. Big mistake.

Had I invested time, effort and energy in my client, communicated with them, inspired them to make good decisions about all aspects of the event, and then executed a plan properly, the entire situation could have been handled better. My client deserved a professional, and in 1992, that was not me. My client trusted that I knew how to run an event. Because I failed to service my client ahead of time and find out the specifics of their celebration, the entire event failed and it was my fault. It could have been easy to blame it on the kids at this event, but in reality, it was my fault.

Lesson learned: As a result of my fateful trip to New Orleans in 1992, I gained a strong sense what should be done in order to properly fulfill a client's vision. The seeds of a system were planted. Fast-forward to today, I teach people all over the country the importance of investing time, energy and resources in understanding what it takes to make a client happy. It's amazing what simple things like listening and communicating will do. Through workshops and speaking engagements I teach others how to inspire their clients; not sell them a host of services, but rather act as a consultant to prospective clients and advise, educate and provide a professional opinion. We come up with plans together, determine a plan of action as a partnership, and work as a team. Then, with time invested and an understanding of my clients' visions of their events, I execute a plan of action. My job is not to execute to their satisfaction, but rather to execute *excellently.*

It all started that day in New Orleans. To date, at each and every event I perform (and there have been well over 2,000 since then) I have one specific goal. NEVER let New Orleans happen again. New

Orleans keeps me humble, keeps me sharp and has provided me with plenty of motivation since 1992, allowing me to be the best at servicing my clients. At the time it was a horrible situation. Looking back I see the tremendous value it offered me in shaping my future.

Business is not just about delivering products or services to a client. It goes way beyond money, contracts, systems, calls, emails and the bottom line. It's about people and a buying experience. I'm not sure when the word "service" came out of customer service. Maybe it was when phone systems automated, the internet became mainstream, when customer service was outsourced overseas or when smart phones exploded on the market. It could have been when Journey lost Steve Perry or when Coke changed its recipe. I don't know for sure, but somewhere along the way, there was a disconnect. Great customer service today seems to be the exception to the rule.

One call to my credit card company proves my point. As is the case for most credit card companies, when I called customer service to dispute a charge I was greeted by an automated system. "Please enter your 16 digit number followed by the pound sign." I entered my 16 digit number, hit the tic tac toe thingy and waited to be connected. "Please press 2 for billing, press 3 to report a lost card...." I quickly hit the "0" deciding that I needed to speak to a human being. "Invalid entry. Please listen carefully as our menu options have changed. Press 2 for billing, press 3 to report a lost card." And so on. Finally hearing the option that I needed, I hit the number 6 button, and was allowed to talk to a customer service representative. With the next 'click' I could tell I was being catapulted to a bustling call center, with dozens, if not hundreds, of other customer service reps. With his headset microphone just a bit too close to his mouth and his volume turned up a little too high, he started his script, "Thank you for waiting, my name is Jerry, can you please give me your name and your 16 digit account number?" All I kept thinking was, *I've already given your automated system my number*, so I questioned the service rep. "For security purposes sir, may I please have your 16 digit number." I yielded and gave up my number. "Thank you, Mr. Sandler, may I call you Dough?" I would have been happy to have him call me *Doug*, but he pronounced it like *dough*, and I was not feeling like a frozen pizza that day. Again I yielded, because all I wanted to do was fix my issue and get on with my day.

"Dough, for additional security, can you please tell me the name of your first girlfriend?" You've got to be kidding me, so of course I questioned Jerry again. "Dough, when you initially set up your security level you decided to use this as your security question." And so I gave him the name of the only girl I can remember from 4th grade. "Thank you, Dough, that is correct." I was actually waiting for Jerry to say, "Please wait while I connect you with her."

Keep in mind, I have not even gotten to the dispute and already I have spent 5 plus minutes on the phone working through security like I am an operative heading through Checkpoint Charlie. Finally I had my chance to state my case for the dispute. "Dough, please hold no more than 3 minutes while I escalate this to my manager." True to his word Jerry returned to the call in 3 minutes with a 'click'. "Dough, I am not able to honor your request." Continuing and obviously reading from a script, Jerry educated me about the terms of my credit card agreement, page 32, paragraph 1, letter A. Who the heck reads a 75-page credit card agreement? I said to Jerry, "Can you do me a favor?" My voice softened. "Can you put down your script for a moment, and talk to me like a human being. Let's talk about this, person-to-person."

I didn't win my dispute without a huge hassle, and I spent far too much time resolving the matter. Companies like my credit card company will eventually find out the hard way that today's customers need better service, stronger relationships and more than ever to feel the love.

There needs to be a shift and a reconnection to customers. It is not acceptable to expect to make a full-time living anymore with half-assed effort. Customers demand and deserve more. Technology should be used as a tool, not as a crutch. Too often, people hide behind technology, firing off an e-mail or zipping off a text, instead of picking up the phone or having a face-to-face meeting or direct dialogue. Technology makes it too easy to hide. It's time to stop hiding and start servicing. I can't recall anyone ever saying they lost a deal because they serviced their clients too well. Start exceeding expectations and leave satisfactory service to your competition.

As you continue reading, the upcoming chapters consist of ways (no secrets) in which you will be able to control the only thing you have control over, and that is you. My goal is to help you understand the importance of "loving up" on your customers, communicating effectively with them and understanding that service is more than just saying yes with a smile. There is a strong correlation between outstanding customer service, strong relationships and the bottom line. I will show you how taking your eye off the money will actually make you more money. Old-school sales techniques (selling features and benefits, overcoming objections and throwing one-liners) don't work because customers today are more educated, savvy and knowledgeable than ever before. Because of technology, they probably know more about your products and services than you do. The stronger your relationships with your prospects and your customers, the easier your job will actually become.

Action Items

1. When in doubt, pick up the phone and call your clients or go visit them. Do not hide behind technology. Nothing beats direct communication.

2. Write down an experience where you feel you were being treated as a number instead of a person. Your goal is to avoid this type of relationship with your customer.

3. List 3 ways in which you think you could improve your level of service with your customer. Keep in mind, exceeding expectations is the goal.

CHAPTER 2

NICE GUYS LEARN TO USE TECHNOLOGY AS A TOOL

The advance of technology is based on making it fit in so that you don't really even notice it, so it's a part of everyday life.

~Bill Gates

Hundreds, probably thousands of books have been written on the advances in technology over the last 30 plus years. For me, because of its model and inspiration, the book *Steve Jobs* stands as a great chronicle. Walter Isaacson conducted many interviews with the late Steve Jobs and his team, his competition and his contemporaries. Jobs, Apple founder and entrepreneur, created an environment where changes in technology were the new normal. In the book, Jobs and his team discuss in detail how technology and Job's obsession for perfection helped define the digital age. Job's passion helped shaped six industries—personal computing, music, animated movies, phones, tablet computing and digital publishing.

Think about your daily activities as they relate to technology, and you will understand the importance of each and every device, program and app. Without each of these digital tools, business today would be completely different. Cell phones, e-mail and personal computers are in our lives to stay. We are connected to others via messaging, smart phones and e-mail. They are three cornerstones of today's digital connections.

As I write this chapter, Washington Talent Agency, the agency that represents my DJ business, has been brought to all but a standstill while a virus is cleared off of its server. Since the phone system is also tied into the computer system via the Internet, calls cannot be made or received. E-mail systems and accounting systems are not functioning yet. And while it is just a matter of a few days since the problem occurred and slated to be repaired in the next 24 hours, it makes you realize exactly how dependent we are on technology to live productive lives.

Small and mid-size businesses are not the only victims. On November 30, 2013 when Christmas retail shopping was kicking into high gear, shoppers in 1,797 of Target's retail stores were not only giving their credit card numbers to the retail giant, but also to digital thieves who hacked into Target's servers earlier that month. Since the breach, analysts estimate that Target will spend billions of dollars on the cleanup.

Using technology, however can be both a blessing and a curse to us. It keeps us connected to everyone and everything. In the grocery store our smartphones help us keep track of our grocery list and coupons but also make it impossible to retreat from our work lives for a moment of peace. While at our desks our customers have easy access to us via e-mail while the same grocery store we were just shopping in sends us our weekly newsletters and coupons to peruse.

As a writer and blogger, I am often asked to write about customer service experiences that I have personally had and the lessons learned from these experiences. Part of the problem is that we are all so connected we don't know exactly how to disconnect. If and when we disconnect, we forget just how important it is to reconnect.

This past year, I wrote a blog titled, "Who gets to see the Wizard?" In my blog, as a service provider, I talk about the importance of the "reconnection."

Do you ever get the feeling your service providers (The Wizard) don't actually want to talk to you? Do the words "Nobody gets to see the Wizard no way, no how" have meaning to you? Phone automation, voicemail and computer technology make it tough to reach another human being. For many, keeping a comfortable arm's distance away from their customers seems to be ok. I say "not ok."

In Chapter 1, I recall a phone call to my credit card company that resulted in lost time, frustration and poor service created by technology, menu options, voice recognition and hold time before a real person, at a call center, picked up and proceeded to ask me the same questions I had just answered via their automated system.

Credit card companies and utility providers are easy targets because they are notoriously lacking any positive level of customer service. In their marketing efforts they stress how important we are to them, but in reality, many fail to provide satisfactory service. And it is rare that any provide exemplary service.

Mega companies don't corner the market on poor service. Much smaller service providers are just as guilty. Examples of local service gone bad include your landscaping guy that has a filled voicemail or your car dealership's busy signal when you are ready for an oil change. It could be your local bank branch's lack of response when you need a question answered, but all you get is voicemail.

If the words "Put him in voicemail" are your friend, I am talking to you. Stop doing it. It's hurting you, your reputation, your business and your bottom line. You may not feel it today because you are busy. But we, the little guys, will remember. And when given a choice to jump ship over pricing, better features or simply a return phone call from your competition, we will do it, quickly and without regret. As a matter of fact, we may wave bye-bye to you and smile as we are waving.

Don't get me wrong, voicemail and phone automation are valuable tools and, if used properly, can increase productivity, improve time management and create a professional environment. But, many times, they are not being used properly. Rather than a tool, it is being used as a weapon to guard against human contact. The very thing being avoided is the one thing that needs to be embraced. The Wizard is human, just like us. But we need to pull back the curtain and reveal him.

A Change in How We do Business

Advances in technology have changed the way we do business. In 1994 I took a sales job working for a company called Standard Register. At the time, Standard Register was known as a forms company. My biggest clients were tool giant Black and Decker, USF&G Insurance, Allied Signal and Maryland Department of Motor Vehicles. My best sellers? Paper forms, multi-part documents and secure documents. I would meet regularly with buyers of these products, count inventory in a stockroom and visit assembly line workers who used our forms.

Today, the forms giant, is still in business. Looking at its website, it is obvious the business has changed with the times. Had they remained in the "paper" business, they would surely have gone the way of the dinosaur. They now have systems in place to help customers with marketing, communications and social media. Standard Register headlines on its webpage a program called Digital Direct Marketing that offers services including QR coding, e-mail initiatives and other forms of web marketing. These changes make it possible for them to stay in business and grow with the digital world we are in today. Just

20 years ago, none of these programs were in place, and at the rate it is going, in another 20 years today's technology will be outdated as well, and companies that fail to change with the times will fail to exist.

Marketing 101 Has Changed

If you are not in tune to marketing your products and services on the web you are falling behind and it is time to catch up. Although we are all in a business of building relationships, it is critical to have technology working for you. For some of you, you have bits and pieces of the equation already in place. For others, marketing today's way will be a complete 180-degree turn from where you were years ago. Above all, I would stress that you should not try to learn everything before you get started. The more you learn, the thirstier you will become since web marketing is an endless proposition. Many books, blogs and articles have been written about using technology to market your product or service. I would advise you start simple, don't get overwhelmed, and find an approach that you are comfortable with using.

Marketing can take the form of direct e-mail communication to a prospective customers, a social media campaign, or if you like writing as I do, maybe you will have a blog that will help educate others while you are updating people with similar interests on the latest trends in your industry.

Here are a few vital components of your marketing campaign:

Your List

Before you do any marketing or promotion of your products or services, you will need a list. It's a must have. Not having a list is the equivalent of opening up a store off a busy highway but not telling anyone about it. No one will visit, and certainly no one will buy your goods. Why would they? Potential visitors know nothing about you yet. Since they don't know you, no one trusts you.

On a piece of paper, draw a large target. The target should have three circles, one inside the other. On the center ring of the target write down everyone you know personally. And I mean everyone, including family and friends. Do not qualify these people in your head. If you are thinking "They will never buy or even have a need for what I am selling," just calm down a moment. I am not asking you to sell anything to them. I just want their names in the center circle.

On the next ring of the target, list all of your close business connections. Current suppliers, current customers, people in your business world. List the business connections that you know. These are people inside and outside your industry and include vendors, association contacts, nonprofits that you come in contact with and people in your line of business. This part of the target includes names of people that would know you if they heard your name.

Finally, the outer ring would include anyone that has ever handed you a business card or that you met at networking event. Collect cards, names and especially e-mail addresses moving forward of anyone that you think would be a good person to know. As I stated earlier, do not focus on them buying your products or services. They may never buy a single thing from you. So why add them to your list? Because they might KNOW someone that wants what you have, and by including them on your list you are adding to your chances of selling something to someone they know. Let the masses be your walking billboard.

I can't emphasize enough the importance of having a good list. It doesn't matter the size of your list. Quality over quantity. I'd rather have a list of 25 names of people that are good quality people than

500 names of individuals you have never met and have no clue who you are or what you do. Your list is the starting point for your entire marketing program. You goal is to continually update and grow your list. Minimum information you should have for any/all names is an e-mail address and first and last name. A phone number or physical address could be very helpful for your use as well.

So now that you have your list together (keep improving and adding to your list), it's time to get information in the hands of everyone on your list. Remember, earlier I said you are looking to share information. You never know who needs what you have, so it's best to share information with people and let them share it with others.

Your Website

If you don't have a website today, you need to get busy. It's easier than you think. No longer do you need to understand HTML code to get your business on the Internet. A simple template website, personalized with your information can be very effective. By following a simple system of filling in the blanks, you can look professional, reach out to a specific segment of the population and promote your products and services.

There are hundreds of companies in place today that create templates for your use. For a small monthly fee you can build your own website, chock full of pictures, links, offerings, documents and more. Companies like Go Daddy, Square Space and countless others make your company look and feel professional with your content.

Social Media Outreach

Facebook, Twitter, LinkedIn, Instagram, Pinterest and many other social media sites will help you spread your message. The key to using any of these sites is to be consistent about it. Don't post 10 updates today, go silent for 2 weeks and post a few more updates every now and again. Make sure you stay top of mind with anyone reading, viewing or commenting on your updates. That means be consistent with how often you update your social media sites. Keep it personal, yet professional on these sites.

There is an easy to read, simple guide to follow called *Social Media Marketing for Dummies* by Shiv Singh and Stephanie Diamond. In the book the authors explain the steps needed to understand, design and launch a social media campaign utilizing many of the social media sites in place today including Twitter, Facebook, YouTube, Google, LinkedIn and others. In addition, the book helps you analyze and measure the effectiveness of your campaign, common mistakes made when launching a social media campaign and key information about how to reach influencers in your market. I would highly suggest you pick up a copy of this guide.

As of the publication of this book, here is a list of FREE (or low fee) online sites that can ease your marketing burden, help you be more productive, increase efficiency and help grow your bottom line. I encourage you to make them a part of any online campaigns you develop.

MailChimp - Online email marketing solution to manage contacts, send emails and track results. Offers plug-ins for other programs.

Wufoo - an online form builder that helps you create contact forms, design online surveys and process simple payments.

Hootsuite - Social media management site.

Vimeo - Online community for storing and distributing video content.

DropBox - Online services that lets you bring your photos, docs, and videos anywhere and share them easily.

A Common Oversight

Whatever you do, never forget that you are dealing with people (much more on this topic later). The key to your business is not perfecting the use of technology or learning the best social media approach to use. But instead, the key is developing relationships. If you have a choice to send an e-mail or make a personal face-to-face connection, choose the latter. Human contact, relationship building and treating people like they are people, not machines, is critical. If there is one thing you should be taking away from this book overall, it is that it is imperative you develop new relationships with people, provide them with one-on-one contact and never lose sight of the fact that people want to deal with people, not machines.

Action Items

1. Develop your target list to include everyone you know. The best way to get word on the street about your products and services is to start with these people.

2. Write down your goals relating to a marketing campaign. Establish or update your website to be more current, and determine which social media channels are best for you.

3. Educate yourself about the basics of today's technology. Change with the times or you will be left behind. It's not realistic to think you will know everything, but it is essential to start educating yourself or your competition will leave you in the dust.

CHAPTER 3

NICE GUYS PUT CUSTOMERS FIRST

There is only one boss. The customer. And he can fire everybody in the company from the chairman on down, simply by spending his money somewhere else.

~Sam Walton

Think about the last exceptional customer service experience you had and what it was that made the experience so incredible. It takes a village to create a culture that puts the customer first. However, exceptional experiences can be created by the efforts of just one person. It may only take one person's world class actions to make a raving fan. Conversely, one bad experience can burn down the same village, and on a larger scale, business practices centered on sales numbers first and customer service second opens the door for less than satisfied clients.

Companies that rely upon sales volume over quality of service, have poorly trained call centers, or a scripted sales force will eventually fail. Prospects do not want to be sold. Instead, they want to buy on their terms. Today's savvy customers rely upon the Internet more and more for company reviews, product investigation and insight as to the best products and services to invest in. Post sale, customer service couldn't be more important than it is today. You can be selling a great product, but if the service is poor you will lose a customer.

Companies should not be fooled by short-term profits; their goal should not be on just selling products. They should strive to create an incredible customer experience, provide essential information in a timely manner and allow the customer to make buying decisions once they feel products and services match their needs.

As an owner of an entertainment company and a speaking business, I train, consult and coach others as well. I am constantly emphasizing the importance of exceptional customer service. A phone call or face-to-face meeting is a great start, but getting into the head of your customer is the only way to create an exceptional experience.

Experiences begin with understanding what and how your customer thinks. However, to really get to the core of what and how they think, you first have to understand WHY your customers think the way they do. You are striving to create an experience that goes well beyond selling products and services to your customer. The end result of a positive experience may be a sold product, but if done properly, you have gotten to know the WHY your customers have in their head. Anyone can have a meeting, but someone who cares will deliver an experience. Understand the WHY, create an exceptional experience for your customer and you will have customer for life.

I have a friend, Mike Gordon, who owns a local music store. Mike grew up around music and is one of those guys who is cool right to the core. As an incredible guitar player and drummer, Mike lives, eats, breathes and sleeps music. He loves watching music videos of awesome guitar players and rock concerts, and he understands what is on the minds of every kid and adult that walks into his store—everyone wants to be a rock star. So Mike (with the help of his extremely creative wife,

Haley) created so much more than a music store.

Before you even step foot in the store you can see the guitar shaped, neon-like sign outside the shop along the roofline. The lights are like beacons, directing the way for wannabe rockers to come take a closer look inside. Once inside the store you feel like a rock star in a green room. There are plush leather chairs, comfy pillows, huge flat screen TV sets and more "please touch" electric guitars within reach than a guy should be allowed to have in one spot. Everything about the store screams, "So you wanna be a rock star?"

The rehearsal rooms look like recording studios. There's a stage where kids can act out their favorite rock and roll tricks, more leather chairs, a huge sofa and art hanging everywhere. Mike's Music creates an experience for young and old. From the moment you meet one of their staffers, teachers, Mike or Haley (or either of their two young girls), you know you are in for a great experience. Mike's huge smile is only outdone by his wife Haley's even bigger smile. They understand the importance of creating a memorable experience for all of their customers. When I first met Mike and Haley, I knew I was in for something special. The public agrees with me and business has been booming since their doors opened several years ago. Mike's Music has expanded their retail floor, lesson rooms, rental business and their market, and I am sure it's just a matter of time before they undergo their next expansion. In addition, Mike's has won community service awards and also has been noted as a "Best of" in local publications.

Mike is not short of competition. Within five miles there are no less than five competitors. But given the competition's offerings of lessons in dingy rehearsal rooms, sitting on folding chairs while waiting for your lesson or your kid, bitter coffee brewed early that morning and a staff that is too cool for school (and they let you know it), it's no wonder the market is flocking to Mike's Music.

A culture like Mike's started with Mike's dream and a vision to one day open a music store and to create an exceptional music experience. Mike understands the importance of knowing the WHY for each and every customer that walks through the door. But you do not need to own a company to make a big impact. Never underestimate the power of one. Know that whatever your position within an organization, you have the ability to win over a customer. And since I am a big believer in the "go big or go home" philosophy, I would suggest you do everything within your power to develop a plan to keep your customers for life. Your plan should start with you. Leave it to your competition to provide satisfactory service. When rating customer experience and customer service on a scale of 1 to 10, you want your score to be a 12.

If the focus of your organization remains where it should, on the customer experience, your organization is moving in the right direction. Every initiative, every service, every mission should be focused on making sure the customer experience is clearly defined and positive. The most successful companies in the world are companies that truly understand they would be out of business without their customers. Those that focus on the bottom line only are missing the point of their existence—to serve the customer.

On a large scale, companies that create the best buying experiences are usually most profitable and top the positive corporate culture list too. They also have leadership that understands mid-level management and rank and file staffers as well. Most importantly, these companies understand their customers. It's no wonder these companies are leaders in their markets. Recognizable names like Apple, Disney, Google and Nike top the list.

Posted on Google's website is "The Top Ten Things We Know To Be True." Item number one proves the point. "Since the beginning, we've focused on providing the best user experience possible. Whether we're designing a new Internet browser or a new tweak to the look of the homepage, we take great care to ensure that they will ultimately serve you, rather than our own internal goal or bottom line."

So whether you are fortunate to have met people like Mike and Haley Gordon or have dealt with a huge company like Google, they are successful because they have put the customer first. But it's one thing to say you will put the customer first and another to actually do it. I created a short list of ways to create an exceptional experience. I have found there are four characteristics common among people and companies big and small delivering exceptional customer experiences. Use these points as your guide to creating an environment of positive vibes, amazing service and ultimately to create an environment where the customer comes first.

1. *Exceed Expectations* – There is a sign taped to my computer that reads, "Set unrealistic expectations, and exceed them." The opposite of this would be, over promise and under deliver. Always fulfill your promises to your customers. Always. If you promise to call your customer back in 5 minutes, call them back in 3 minutes. If you tell your prospect you are going to have a proposal delivered in 24 hours, get it to them in an hour. Challenge yourself to follow through on every promise, return every phone call, answer every question presented to you and do it all with a smile and a thank you. Remember, perception is your customer's reality. If you take the philosophy of being responsible for everything relating to the customer you are well on your way to exceeding expectations. Too often, people try to pass the buck. If the buck stops with you, you are doing it right.

2. *Be Consistent* – Consistency equates to predictable results. If I am a customer, the last thing I am looking for is a surprise (unless of course I am getting extra value as well). I want a product or service that is reliable and that I can count on. Consistency is like a promise kept.

In exchange for my hard earned dollar, you are providing a service that I need and expect. People talk, and that's a good thing (or bad, depending on how well you service your clients). Others talking about the amazing service you provide will help you get more referrals and more business. But if your service runs hot and cold, depending on your mood or the day of the week, you are not going to win. The best way to be consistent is to work within the guidelines of a system. My system of Invest, Inspire and Execute follows in an upcoming chapter. I encourage you to use it, take ownership of it and make it a habit in your life. When dealing with your customers, the bottom line is, they want to be treated fairly, consistently and exceptionally.

3. *Inspire and Wow Them* – Your wowed clients are your most profitable clients and the ones that will buy from you again and again. Plus, if you wow a client they will be your biggest referral source. But, in order to wow them, you need to stop selling and start consulting. Turn a meeting into a one-on-one consultation. Once you stop selling and start advising, the magic will begin. You will be at your best and accomplish most when a client trusts you and follows your advice. Stop focusing on closing a deal and collecting a check and start focusing on answering questions and genuinely helping your client. But remember, you are the expert and although you probably know everything about your product or service, there is no need to tell them all you know. I refer to this as "puking product." It is critical to keep in mind this is not about you, it's about them.

4. *Get Personal* – The phrase "it's only business" is incorrect. Let me go one step further and say it's never *just* business. You want your client to like you. Not just as a vendor, but as a person. People want to do business with people they like, and they want to feel as though they are your only client. Being personal is essential; being present during every conversation and meeting is critical. Put down the smartphone, put your ringer on silent and focus on every word your client is saying.

If they mention something about their oldest child in college, make a mental note. If you come across a news article or blog about the school, send them the link. Make time to understand the elements that make your client "tick." What inspires, motivates and makes your clients truly happy? Get personal and the business will follow.

Invest the time needed to exceed expectations, to be consistent, to develop a relationship and to wow your client. If you ever question why you lost your last customer or failed to close the deal, review the list of four actions above. You may have missed one or all of the actions on the list. Gain trust, understand your clients, help them fix their problems, and they will stay loyal to your business.

When you create an exceptional buying experience you are tapping into the emotions of your customer while creating a lifelong positive experience full of pleasant memories for them as well. People will gladly pay top dollar when you add value to the buying process in addition to creating great memories along the way. Furthermore, you are creating an atmosphere of trust as you forge a deeper connection with your customer.

Action Items

1. Write down your customer's WHY. Why do they need what you are offering/selling them? If you are in doubt, ask several customers about their WHY.

2. Rate your level of service on a scale of 1 to 10. Anything short of 10 needs to be improved upon. List how you can improve upon your customer's buying experience.

3. List 5 ways in which you could WOW your customer and provide over-the-top service.

CHAPTER 4

NICE GUYS USE SYSTEMS

Life is really simple, but we insist on making it complicated.

~Confucius

If I had to select a chapter in this book that contains the framework for my system and the process I use today, it would be this one. I can't stress enough the importance of using systems as a way of life. Systems are designed for success and to simplify a process. Albert Einstein said, "Everything must be made as simply as possible. But not simpler." If you design an easy to use system, remade, revised and refined through trial, tribulation and error, and are consistent with its use, your process will become a habit. Good habits, when combined with good systems, will create winning results.

Systems are everywhere in life. Simply put, systems are a group of related parts that work together. They can be used in every aspect of life. There are systems designed to help you raise kids, to teach you how to drive a car and to help you sell hamburgers. Probably the most famous system in place today is McDonald's. Two all beef patties, special sauce, lettuce, cheese, pickles, onions on a sesame seed bun. I can hear the jingle playing in my head. If you drive down any main street in your town, chances are good you will see a McDonald's restaurant. The Golden Arches are the same color no matter where in the world you see them, PMS Pantone color 123 Yellow, with a Red PMS Pantone color 485 background.

Walking into any McDonald's you will discover that many, if not all of the characteristics of the McDonald's you are standing in, are similar from location to location. Menu options are the same. Coffee temperature is the same. Restaurant layout and fixtures are the same with very few exceptions, no matter where you are in the world.

The McDonald's Corporation works diligently at putting systems in place. In 1961 they created Hamburger University as a way to teach franchise owners the systems used at all of their restaurants. The university, situated on 80 acres, maintains 13 teaching rooms and 3 kitchen labs and can teach classes in 28 different languages. Thousands attend the university each year. McDonald's, one of the most successful franchises in history today, invests in systems, and so should you.

You don't have to be a fast-food giant or multi-billion dollar company to benefit from systems. Systems are designed for many reasons, but the key reason systems exist in the business world is to support and make efficient all of the activities within an organization. Systems will help us determine what and when we are doing something wrong as well. Systems, if set up properly, help us not just determine good processes but also help us measure productivity and efficiency. The goal of any business system put in place is to help your organization get positive results.

When I started my business, I wanted to succeed. I didn't necessarily know how I was going to get there, but I hoped I would be successful. With my DJ business, I started small and put a procedure in place to make just 3 phone calls a day to venues or agencies that hired talent for their events. Although it was a simple goal, I had to make these calls during my lunch hour at my full-time job or in the evenings when I got home. I made it a goal to get to one networking event a month, read one self-help business book a month and to turn off the car radio and listen to a business type audiobook while driving instead.

Quickly, I was hooked and new habits started to form. If I got in the car and an audiobook wasn't with me, I would miss the learning time. Since I told others about my goal to make 3 phone calls a day to grow my DJ business, I'd have co-workers at my full-time job remind me to make my calls if they saw me idle during lunch time. My "system" consisted of reading books, making phone calls and attending networking meetings. I remained consistent (see my chapter on consistency), developed good business habits and worked hard in the spare time I had to build my DJ business. In 1999, I succeeded in taking my DJ business from a part-time hobby to a full-time job. The dream was a GO!

Since then, I have made it my practice to put systems in place for everything I do in business. Social media marketing campaigns, e-mail blasts, phone campaigns, client follow-up communication and everything related to customer service. And although I have systems in place, nothing is so rigid that I can't bend the rules a bit to allow for the human element. The worst excuse for using a business practice or system is "because it has always been done this way." You should always allow for change in your system because change is what will improve the process you have in place. Fleetwood Mac band member and accomplished singer songwriter, Lindsay Buckingham, said, "If you are any good at all, you know you can be better." And although systems and processes were developed and designed for success, be open to change them to improve the systems you created.

When I created my Nice Guys Finish First speaking platform, business system and process, I designed it based upon a three simple elements:

1. Invest (my time, my energy, my resources)

2. Inspire (my customer to take action, become their consultant)

3. Execute (our plan excellently)

We are all in the P.R. business—people and relationships. Don't get confused, or think just because your company sells office supplies, that you are in a business of staplers and ink. If you are a part of the insurance business, your company does far more than collect premiums and pay out benefits. And, if you sell cars, you are definitely not in the business of selling transportation. You are in the business of people and relationships, and without them, your business will fail. It is up to you to strengthen the bond you have with your customer, or you will be seen as a commodity. Commodities are easily replaced. People are not.

When you get approached by a customer looking for you to solve a problem, regardless of whether you sell pencils, health benefits or vehicles, they first look at you as a person. At initial glance, your customer is sizing you up, trying to determine if they trust you and if they do, if they should also follow your advice. If you deal with people over the phone, you are being judged by your tone, the speed at which you are speaking and your volume level. The words you say, the body language you share and information you offer are all under a microscope. Regardless of being face-to-face with a customer, over the phone or via email (which has its own set of challenges), you are being judged. Customers think, "Do I trust this person? Do I like this person? Will he give me the right advice?"

Each element (invest, inspire and execute) is designed to improve the relationship, strengthen the bond, and build the connection that I have with my client or prospective client. My three step system is a way for me to stay focused on a process and not let the sometimes emotional side of selling and servicing get in my way. The system is designed to keep me on track.

As a part of servicing a client properly, it is essential to invest time in our clients in order to understand their full set of needs. It's very challenging to get to know people, build a relationship, and help them make decisions and execute a plan excellently unless we have invested ourselves in understanding them. Invested time equates to phone calls, meetings, e-mails, text messaging, face-to-face get-togethers and any other level of communication used in building the relationship. Keep in mind, each instance of communication does not necessarily have to be business related. One of the best people I know at selling and servicing clients routinely has breakfast "appointments" with clients and prospects. During breakfast, he has one rule that he strictly follows. The rule is that he will not discuss business unless his breakfast partner initiates the conversation. It's genius and so simple. As a result, he knows everything about the person he is eating with including where their kids go to college, upcoming milestone celebrations and lots of other personal things. He has become a master at rapport building. Of course if the client starts talking business, he will chime in and provide information, but within no time, he is back to talking about their personal plans on life and the future. I have had an opportunity to meet with some of these people, and when I ask what they like most about his style the answer is always the same. "He really knows me." "He communicates with me, so I can follow what he is talking about." "He gets me." The best answer that I have heard is, "I really feel like he cares about me, and although I know I am a client, our relationship goes much further than that. We are friends." Bingo, that is exactly what you are looking for in order to be successful—a relationship in which your client doesn't just think you care, they KNOW you care.

Make the most of your customer's time and attention. Early in my career as a high schooler, I worked at The Great Cookie selling cookies from behind a counter. As customers approached the counter, I would focus attention completely on them, create an environment where I was 100% present during our conversation, provide them with a great tasting product and carry the sale from inception to completion in less than 60 seconds in most cases. Service with a smile, eye contact and helpful suggestions or information was paramount. I invested a proper amount of my resources in order to successfully fulfill my customer's goal of buying cookies.

Still early in my career, as a mortgage loan officer, investing my time, energy and resources became a 60-day process, not a 60-second process like the cookie business. In the mortgage business, face-to-face meetings, calls to third party agents, processors, real estate professionals and others became my time investments. That was just the minimum that I required from myself. Those investments were a part of the job. Being new to the world of service, I would push myself to get to know my clients. As I invested time in my clients, I started to learn about their "why." In depth, detailed conversations were about why they were buying a house, how they picked the neighborhood they decided to move to and what their plans were for their future. Just like my friend who has breakfast meetings, I was beginning to develop strong connections with my clients. Several clients that I established in the mortgage business have used me as an entertainer for their milestone events, currently read my blog and highly anticipated the release of this book so they could find out more about my Nice Guy system.

There is a great quote by Zig Ziglar. "You can get everything you want in life if you will just help enough other people get what they want." Your job is to help others get what they want. To do that, you must help them make decisions and choices. The better relationships you have established and the closer the bond between you and your customer, the more comfortable they will feel with you. Your advice, guidance and leadership will help inspire them to take action. As your relationship grows, magic will happen and you will become a trusted advisor and consultant. As a consultant, you become their paid professional. I love the feeling of working with a client to help them reach their goals. If you focus less on the money you are making and more on your client, the money will come.

As a business consultant and service expert, I love when I feel that "click" between me and my client. The click is called trust. At that point, they know that I have their best interest at heart when I am providing them advice. For example, as a part of one of the workshops that I give, when talking about client's budget I use a slide that says, "Just because you know your client's budget does not mean you have to use it all." If your clients trust you, they will feel confident in the advice you are providing and the magic will occur. Your perspiration from investing time, energy and resources, when combined with the trust you have gained from your investment will put you in the perfect place and set the ideal conditions for inspiring your prospect or customer to take action.

My mom once said to me something that has forever stayed in my head. "You can land a plane 90% correct and still kill everyone onboard." If you invest the resources in your client and inspire them to take action, but either fail to launch your plan or fail at carrying out your plan properly, you will fail at producing successful results. Essential in the process is the third step of the system—execute. To be truly successful you must execute excellently. Make your goal more than just closing a deal, one more dial or crossing an item off the list. Don't miss an opportunity to build a relationship and go above and beyond. My goal is to consistently set unrealistic expectations and exceed them. Every. Single. Time. You are in business to help others, as Zig Ziglar says. Work hard to help others get what they want.

As an entertainer, I work hard to arrive at event date well prepared and ready to go. One to two years of planning, preparation and decision making all come to a fulcrum on event day. Each and every item on the list that I discuss with my client including lighting, music selection, volume level, timing and minute details happens within a small window of time on event date. It is very important for me to understand all of the details and execute our plan, excellently. To achieve a rating of "satisfactory" is not nearly good enough. If you are anything like me, good is not good enough. I am looking for excellence in my execution. Since I have built a relationship with my client, it is no longer something that I only want to do, it is something that I must do. I owe it to my client. I take every event date very personally. Although I am a "vendor" at the event, I'd much rather consider myself (as my client would as well) as the professional in charge, so they won't have to be.

I focus all of my effort on event day on making sure the experience is exceptional for my client. As I carry out the plan, I think back to each bit of time I invested in my client, inspiring them to make decisions on each component that is brought to life on event date, and making sure each is precisely aligned with their vision as we discussed it. Although things on event day can be adjusted to fit the exact environment created at the celebration, my client knows the only reason I would have changed things or adjusted plans was to make it even better than we had originally planned on. Executing excellently is a must, and exceeding expectations creates a plan in which the results 100% of the time will further connect my client with me. My goal for myself is always to retain a customer for life.

The system I have put in place (invest, inspire and execute) was designed to be simple, easy to use, effective and to create huge positive impact on my business. And it will for you too. Regardless of what system you are using today, the key is to take ownership in everything you do, make adjustments where you need to in order to feel comfortable with it and stay with it. Failure to stay within the perimeters of a well thought out system will have you flying by the seat of your pants and unsure of your next move. Our world is filled with plenty of people accepting average results, so make it your responsibility to be one of the exceptional ones.

Action Items

1. Write down the systems you have in place today to help you improve your business. (Do you have a sales system, accounting systems, customer relationship system?)

2. List the improvements you think you could you make in the systems.

3. Set a goal for yourself to make the improvements with an actual date. Hold yourself accountable.

CHAPTER 5

NICE GUYS CREATE A CONSISTENT
PATTERN FOR SUCCESS

Persistence will let you have it. Consistency will let
you own it.

~Doug Sandler

Airline pilots, surgeons, and nice guys have something in common. To be successful in their line of work, all of them must be
consistent. To be fair, in order to be successful, anyone would need to
be consistent, and not just pilots, surgeons and nice guys. Fortunately,
for most people, consistency is not usually a matter of life and death.
The problem with people, however, is that we lack consistency. External influences drive us to be inconsistent. Even the most motivated of
individuals must work hard to instill the proper behaviors to stay consistent. It can take years of schooling, on-the-job training and consistent professional behavior to create a pattern for success. Specifically,
that is why we have co-pilots, assistant surgeons and training systems
in place, to help create a consistent pattern for success.

As an example of inconsistent behavior, if you sell a client on
the idea of using your services, but fail to deliver your products in a

timely manner, you will probably fail to get future business from your customer. At a very minimum, you have harmed the level of trust your client has in you. Failure to deliver as promised has a very negative effect on your business. To make matters worse, a negative client will tell as many as seven people about their negative experience with you.

Your behavior will need to be consistent in order to win additional business from your customer. You need to focus on a new default. The new default will be consistent, positive behavior and exceeding expectations. If you are motivated by negative reinforcement, you have to assume with this new default that something as simple as an unreturned phone call or poor service will lose you a customer.

Notorious for inconsistent customer service or poor service in general, are the large utility and cable companies across the country. Even in the mid-Atlantic there are relatively few choices when it comes to Internet, cell phone, and cable companies, so maybe they feel they have a corner of the market and need not improve. I recently made a call that required a service technician to come to my home. The solution I got from their customer service call center was an appointment over a week away and a choice of an appointment between either 7:30 a.m. and 12:30 p.m. or 12:30 p.m. and 5:30 p.m. A technician could show up anytime within that window. Not liking the answer I was given, I hung up and called back. On my callback, I found an empathetic service rep that managed to "work the system" and set up an appointment for me within 24 hours. Additionally, she gave me an exact time the service tech would be arriving. When I inquired about how she was able to make such an appointment, her response was, "We all have the power to make appointment revisions here, you just have to know how to work the system." Had the first customer service rep focused more time on pleasing me and less time on getting to the next phone call, she also could have had a happy customer. Inconsistent behavior within a team is trouble.

It wasn't until I started to work for myself and rely upon my business as a way to support myself and my family that I truly began to understand the importance of consistency as it pertains to my business.

It was May of 1998 and I received a phone call from a friend of mine who at the time ran a small talent agency in Baltimore. Lois told me about a local association that wanted to put together a fun meeting involving a game show. Since Lois knew I was always up for something new, I asked her two questions. "How much time do I need to fill, and how much money will I be making?" I probably asked her in the reverse order since I was always so focused on making money. Lois explained that I needed to fill about 40 minutes of time and would be paid about $300 for the work. Later I would realize the forty minutes I was about to invest in this meeting and the paycheck I made that night would be worth millions of dollars over the next fifteen plus years.

Although the money they were about to pay me was low, the gig was on a weeknight and I was up for the fun and games. After a short call to the association member planning this event, I discovered the program was for a group of industry people including party planners, talent agents, catering executives and business owners in event and meeting planning businesses.

When I arrived at the meeting and started setting up, I was approached by a man who introduced himself as Chuck Kahanov. Chuck was a partner of a talent agency in a DC suburb, Washington Talent Agency. Before starting my game show that evening (Chuck had no idea if I was even any good at what I do), he asked me if I was represented by a talent agent. Little did I know, the audition and interview had just begun. I explained to Chuck that I was not, but I was open to talking to him after the meeting. The rest of the story seems like a fairy tale. For nearly 20 years, I have been represented by Washington Talent.

Chuck and I have remained very close friends and he and his partner, Robert Sherman, have taught me about consistency, dependability and reliability. They also taught me about the importance of having an incredible work ethic, which is a missing link in the events industry. I am sure it is also a missing component in other professions as well. Most people in the entertainment business feel that showing up and working a four hour gig means you have a good work ethic. They fail to realize all of the other parts of business are extremely important as well. Here is a short list of some of the things we all need to be consistent about in order to be successful:

The Magic List of Consistency

- Returning phone calls

- Returning e-mails

- Setting realistic expectations

- Following up with prospective clients

- Checking in with your current clients

- Developing and running an effective marketing campaign

- Networking with industry professionals

- Handling your business affairs properly (accounting, PR, marketing, selling, training)

- Maintaining balance between your business and personal life

- Communicating effectively

What I am hoping you get from this list is that there is no magic, smoke and mirrors and nothing complicated about the list. At no point do I mention the need for vast product knowledge or to spend a lot of money on promotions or PR campaigns. Each item on the list is essential and must be handled consistently. Unfortunately, some people will be great at returning calls but horrible with setting realistic expectations with their clients, or they are great at handling accounting, but they have no balance with their personal life. The items on the list are not negotiable, just as being consistent is not negotiable. You can apply this list to any business model in any industry. Consistency is key. Without it, your results will be below average.

I am often asked what the secret is to any success that I have seen over the years. The secret is that there is no secret. Woody Allen is credited with saying, "Eighty percent of success is showing up." And to a certain degree, Woody is right. I revise it this way—One hundred percent of success is showing up again and again, consistently.

I have often found that people are not consistent for a number of reasons. The most prominent reason people are not consistent is because they let life get in the way. They have the best of intentions but somewhere along the way, they get sidetracked. The reasons for getting sidetracked can be as simple as the phone ringing, or it can be as complicated as a failed marriage, a health issue or lack of a solid goal. Life happens, and you can count on it happening to you as well. Here is how I combat this issue and allow myself to move past it. It's not the problem, it's how you deal with the problem that counts.

Once I signed an agreement with Washington Talent to have them represent me, I made one simple set of rules for myself. The top rule on the list is to be consistent in my actions. I made a promise to do everything in my power to follow through on every commitment I made and to be consistent with each of the items on the *Magic List of Consistency.* One hundred percent. Ninety percent was not good enough. I was concerned that any business that I potentially could get from the agency could go to another DJ if I did not follow through 100% of the time.

Lessons Learned in my Childhood

Even though I was not a lover of sports, I wanted some sort of activity in my life when I was still in high school. Maybe that should read that my mom wanted me out of the house and not sitting in front of television every day after school. Either way, I joined the soccer team in 9th grade, and in 10th grade I played on the golf team as well.

As a part of soccer team practice, there were a series of drills that became daily activities before we started the official field practice. The drills included running and kicking the ball around small orange cones, taking shots on goal from the corner of the field and doing dreaded wind sprints along the sidelines.

Although we all thought these drills were boring and an unimportant part of the game (especially the wind sprints), we began to realized these drills instilled consistent habits needed in order to win a game. More importantly, the drills were essential in separating the starters from the guys put on the bench. If we couldn't handle the drills, how would we ever be able to handle the game? We learned this just a few days into the practice season. Those of us that wanted to play in the game worked extra hard at the drills. Coaches were influenced not just by our skill level, but also our drive, our passion and our attitude. The drills also taught us about proper ball handling, strength, endurance and consistency on the field. In order to win, you need to have all of those physical skills plus passion for the game and a great attitude.

As I started to develop my own "skill set" in business, and long before I developed the relationship with Washington Talent Agency, I began to see a consistent pattern for any success I was able to achieve. It didn't take long before I started to understand three key ingredients that helped me close more deals, properly service clients and develop a source for referrals. The rules were easy to follow, and the pattern was predictable. In order to gain confidence from my clients, I discovered I needed to consistently do the following:

- Return every phone call

- Always be a nice guy (my mom was right)

- Always tell the truth

I printed out these rules and kept them on my bulletin board. I would look at them daily. They were staring me in the face when I was on each and every call. I also had them written on a small piece of paper folded up in my wallet. To this day I continue to be a very visual person. If I can see it with my eyes, visualize it in my head and say it out loud, it will be my reality.

As business evolved over the years and I started to teach others, the basic premise of the three ingredients didn't change. As a part of my Nice Guys Finish First program I developed a more comprehensive list for properly servicing customers consistently:

- Return every phone call

- Return every e-mail

- Deliver on every promise

- Be on time, every time

- Keep communication and relationships personal

The program, called the NG30 (NiceGuy30) was developed to create a consistent pattern for action. I developed the program after doing an analysis of my business activities. I discovered that if I kept this as a baseline when dealing with my customers, and was consistent in following these behaviors, I had a head start in the journey to success. We only have control over our own behaviors, we must be consistent about them and create good habits. Tracking your results, new behaviors and forming habits over 30 days, the NG30 program would enable you to follow the same pattern for success that I developed.

Here are the general guidelines:

1. **Calls** - Return every call. Every phone call, no matter who calls, must be returned within 24 hours. If they call you by name and/or you know their name, you need to return their call. That includes salespeople, prospects, friends and anyone else trying to reach you.

2. **E-mails** - Return every e-mail from anyone who addresses you by name. The exception to this would be spam or mass marketed e-mail campaigns. Regardless if your e-mail is short, you must respond the same day.

3. **Promises** - Deliver on every promise you make. "I'll write that memo today" really means you will write that memo today, not tomorrow. If you say it, e-mail it, communicate it or otherwise promise it, it must be done. If you don't think you can fulfill a promise, don't make it.

4. **Be on time** - You must be on time, every time. No exceptions. No excuses for lateness because of traffic, tickets, dental appointments, ostrich sightings or otherwise. Be on time, every time. Period. Yes, 15 minutes late is late. Respect other people's schedules.

5. Communicate Personally - Building relationships is key. Reach out to warm contacts or customers just to say "hello." The key here is you are not allowed to promote your product or service directly unless asked via follow-up. If they ask about business, you are cleared to talk business.

The NG30 program is available free on my website (www. DougSandler.com). My advice would be to print it out, tack it to your bulletin board, and look at it every day. The program will help you regardless of your business. It will remind you of the essential ingredients you will need in order to keep your business moving in the right direction.

To be successful, it is very important that you follow the program guidelines consistently. You must make sure that you follow the 5 steps on a daily basis. If you follow them every other day, or you just follow four of the five, you are greatly reducing your chances for success. For example, if you return all your calls and e-mails, deliver on your promises and you are on time consistently, but you decide ingredient number five (reaching out to others) is not something you are going to do, you will greatly diminish your probability of success. .

Additionally, during a sales call you noticed a family picture on your prospective customer's desk. In the picture the entire family is at Disney. You, being a great communicator and wanting to be relatable, ask your prospect about the trip. As you talk further you discover this was his family's first trip to Disney and the kids loved Epcot.

After you get back to your office, you send a nice follow-up e-mail, or, even better, you send a handwritten note. Nice touch, but let's take it to the next level. A week goes by and you happen to see an article in the newspaper including fun facts related to Epcot and the Magic Kingdom. You clip the article and drop it in the mail to your prospect or you send the article via e-mail. The action of sending the article takes you from being a salesperson to being a human. You are on your way to becoming a "Nice Guy."

Follow each of the program ingredients without fail for 30 days. At the end of 30 days you will discover a set of new habits that will put you on the winning track to consistency and success.

There is no magic formula for winning and no secret code unlocking the door to success. In order to be successful, we need to be consistent in our positive actions. Each element in the success process is essential, and when applied consistently it will lead to positive results.

Action Items

1. Write down a list of actions that you currently feel you are not consistent with pertaining to your business.

2. Write down a list of the actions you need to do daily in order to be successful in your business. This will become your Magic List of Consistency.

3. Download the NiceGuy30 (NG30) guidelines and review them daily for 30 days.

CHAPTER 6

NICE GUYS BUILD TRUST

If people like you, they will listen to you. But if they
trust you, they will do business with you.

~Zig Ziglar

As my career started to take shape, I began to understand that
selling was more about helping others and not only a means to a
paycheck and helping myself. I began to understand the importance of
relationships and the role they play in the selling cycle. I noticed the
more I communicated with my clients, the greater my relationships
with them evolved. As my relationships with my customers grew
deeper, my opinion and voice was more valuable in helping them make
decisions. Along the way, magic happened. Not hocus pocus magic
but even better—a connection that transcended selling. My customers
started to trust me, and I inspired them to make good choices. Gratitude
became a valuable aspect of our relationship. Honesty became the
focus of the relationship, not products, features or benefits. Pricing
was no longer the leading factor of whether or not a sale was made.
And if there was something that I thought was important for my client
to know that was of issue, I considered it my obligation to discuss it
because of our relationship. My customers were counting on me and I
did not want to let them down, under any circumstance.

Without trust, our services become more about the features of the services we provide and less about resolving our customer's problems. Although moving products and services is the ultimate goal, the sale becomes a bi-product of the relationship you have with your customer. When our customer trusts us, the buying cycle becomes more about communication, offering advice, solving a problem and showing gratitude.

Ralph Waldo Emerson said, "Trust men and they will be true to you; treat them greatly and they will show themselves great."

Trust is something earned as a relationship grows and matures. The more your customer feels you are invested in your relationship, the better your chances of gaining trust. If you prove yourself again and again, you will build trust with your client.

Relationships rely upon trust. Success depends on it. Consistently win it and you will be labeled as "worthy." Without it, you will be hard pressed to forge binding connections, and you'll be challenged to find others willing to be loyal to you. Ultimately, unless you are very lucky, you will have difficulty making a living without it. I am talking about trust with a capital T. And that stands for trouble if you don't earn trust. It may seem obvious that building trust is essential to building strong relationships, but to many people it is not so obvious. Relationships built on trust can stand the test of time. What may not be as obvious is how to get others to trust you.

Let me put some velvet on the sledgehammer before I hit you with it. You will never be too experienced, too powerful or too knowledgeable to stop working on building trust. We all need improvement in the category of building trust since we are always working on building relationships with people we meet. The process is dynamic and never complete.

A Test of Trust

Dig deep and do an analysis of yourself to complete this reality check. It's time to measure your level of TRUST. Use the checklist below to see if you are making the grade. Answer each sentence with yes or no. After you complete your test, score yourself as I indicate below the test.

Regarding my relationships:

1. I am 100% reliable

2. I tell the truth

3. I give more than is expected

4. I am always on time

5. I work on resolving problems quickly

6. I am dependable and available to answer questions

7. I see things from their perspective

8. I am consistent with my service

9. I am a part of the solution, not a part of the problem

10. I demonstrate I truly care

11. I make others feel special because they are special to me

12. I am proactive when it comes to providing information and insight

13. I communicate clearly

14. I understand the matters that concern others

15. I follow the golden rule and treat others as I would like to be treated

16. I listen to what others have to say

17. I make others look good

18. I keep confidential information confidential

19. I honor my commitments

20. I work on being all I can be for others

21. I show genuine gratitude and appreciation

22. I always show respect

23. I earn the business

24. I say I am sorry when I am wrong

25. I add value to the relationship

Here's how you score the test. Multiply the number of "yes" answers you have by 4 to get your score. If you scored over 91? Way to go "A" student. You are doing great, keep up the great work and continue to build trust. Score between 80 to 88? Solid score, but work on the "no" responses and take the test again later. If you scored in the 70s or lower, you probably have many relationships that could evaporate quickly unless you focus on improving your relationships and improving on the areas you answered "no." Lifelong relationships develop when you have trust between people. The best way to improve on a low score is to study others that do what you do but have a lot more experience. Read books, listen to audio recordings, read success blogs. Find out what these people have done in order to be successful.

Many companies have gotten away from building their brand on trust. And for a short-term period of time, they probably will be able to get away with it. Companies bend the truth with their claims of products that will make you younger, thinner, happier and cooler. We are so desperate that we believe them. We buy their products by the millions and often times fail to even take it out of the box. If we do use them, we are not surprised when they don't work. We realize that things that seem too good to be true, are usually too good to be true for a reason.

Companies that have built their brand on great service, great value, great products and are consistent over the long run will gain our trust and our business. Warren Buffet says it best. "It takes 20 years to build a reputation and 5 minutes to ruin it." Always stay true to your word, communicate effectively, provide educated advice and great service and you will be well on your way to building a relationship based upon trust.

How to Build Trust

As I became more experienced in selling, building relationships with my customers and servicing, I realized that in order to be successful I needed to turn my approach around. Selling wasn't about me, it was about them. The more I focused on my customer, the more successful I would become. Understanding, having empathy, and gaining perspective became my everyday reality. Each call I would take from a customer, I turned into a practice of empathy. But I also discovered the importance of truly understanding how traits like honesty, conviction and gratitude are tied to building trust. As a result, there are several important factors that need to be a part of any relationship involving trust.

1. *Truth* - Tell the truth even when the results are not favorable for you. Imagine clients buying a product that you know isn't the right fit for them. Over the course of time, you know they will also come to the same conclusion. It's best to lose the short-term sale by telling

your client the truth now. In the long run you will be pleased with the results. You can never go wrong by telling the truth.

2. *Perspective* - As a speaker I have an entire program based upon perspective. Understanding what makes your customers "tick" is essential to building trust. If you understand their problems, concerns and what keeps them up at night, you are doing your job properly. If you have a product or service that can help solve one of their problems, even better. Often times, however, prospective customers may not know what is causing their problem, so asking good questions, being an effective communicator and providing honest advice is a great way to help build trust.

3. *Respect your clients time* – Want a sure fire way to lose a customer? Don't respect their time and you are guaranteed to lose a customer, and you will surely not gain their trust. I have been in a position over the years to hire people and the first thing I tell them about the job is, "Be on time, every time." Arriving late is a huge sign of disrespect and not acceptable. I'd hire someone less talented but more dependable ten out of ten times. Respect is very challenging to teach, but I can teach someone on-the-job talent through training. You are 100% in control of your time and it is essential that you respect your customer's time. To build trust, you are required to show up on time for appointments, do not overstay your time at an appointment, follow through on every promise you make ("I will call you back in 5 minutes" really means that you will call back in 5 minutes or less) and stay in control of your schedule by not overcommitting. Being respectful of your customer's time is so easy to do, yet a component of building trust that is often overlooked when you are not seeing things from your customer's perspective.

4. *Dedication and hard work* - Legendary baseball player Babe Ruth said, "It's hard to beat a person who never gives up." If you believe

in something, it is worth working for. Success is not easy and trust is not given casually. If you stay in the game long enough, people will take notice. If you dedicate yourself and live a life of purpose, people will recognize your dedication and hard work. Thomas Edison said, "There is no substitute for hard work." At any job that I would perform, I worked hard. Regardless of being a DJ, a mortgage officer, real estate agent or a guy that worked in a cookie store, I worked hard. I may not have been the best at any of those positions, but I can guarantee you that no one worked harder than me or was more dedicated to the position than me. Prospects and customers definitely see your effort and trust someone that works hard and is dedicated to his position.

Companies and people that are dedicated to building trust are the most successful. Trust starts with open and honest communication. You will continue to build trust by working hard and staying focused on building an incredible customer experience. If you keep an eye on solving your customer's problems you will continue to build trust and have a happy customer. If issues arise, work hard to resolve them quickly. If your customer feels like you are doing everything you can, they will stay with you because of your dedication to them.

Action Items

1. Write down a list of clients that you want to work harder at gaining their trust.

2. Take the test of trust found within this chapter.

3. List the areas you are going to improve and what steps you will take to improve. Be specific.

CHAPTER 7

NICE GUYS EMPOWER OTHERS

If you don't empower your employees to make decisions, then you will continue to make all of the decisions yourself, and you will never grow beyond that.

~ Strickland Bonner

You can't be in all places at the same time, so if you run a company, manage a group of employees or want to grow beyond where you are now, it is important to let go and let others take control. Knowing when to let go of responsibility is very important.

People are competitive by nature, we often feel no one can do our job as good as us, and we face the push-pull, internal struggle of letting go of the reins. Mentally, we want to hold on because we feel as though when we let go of control, all will be lost, but just the opposite will occur.

As the owner of a company, I am continually working on empowering others to make decisions. And although it is a difficult decision, because I am a control freak, I am learning that if you put the right people in place and empower them to make decisions without micromanaging them, the majority of the time they will make the right decision for your business.

Empowering others is good for a variety of reasons. It's not only good for you as a business owner or someone that manages people, but it is good for your people as well. An empowered workforce is more connected to the company they work for if they are given a chance to make decisions for their company. As a business consultant, I will often watch salespeople who have little control over pricing lose a deal for fear of lowering the price, because they have no control to do so. The same employee, when empowered to make pricing adjustments, treats the customer completely differently. Body language, expressions and how they handle the customer is significantly different for the empowered employee. Giving someone control to adjust pricing or make decisions for the company does not always mean they will lower prices or make an adverse decision.

Too often companies will set up a "false empowerment" program in which they give their employees the ability to make decisions but they micromanage the decisions they make. In essence, the employee works in fear of making the wrong decision, so he makes decisions based upon what he thinks management would want instead of what he thinks would be a good decision. Not only does this type of false empowerment hurt the employee, it significantly affects his role in the company, lowers his productivity and reduces the amount of time he will stay with the company. Imagine working in an environment that allows you to make decisions but is critical of the decisions you make.

It is essential a series of guidelines be given to the employees. People work much more efficiently when they are given a set of expectations to meet.

Guidelines for Setting up a Team of Empowered Employees

- Trust your people

- Leave the line of communication very open

- Set goals that need to be met

- Make sure employees are aware that failing is ok. It's "safe" to fail.

- Recognize accomplishments, give credit to all on the team

- Encourage independence

- Encourage teamwork

- Create an open door policy

- Encourage out-of-the-box thinking and working

Benefits of Empowering Your Team

- Creates a much better team environment

- Breaks down barriers and creates an environment of cooperation

- Employees with think more independently and creatively

- Increased productivity and efficiency

- Employees happier in their roles

- Significantly cuts down office politics and negativity

Benefits Your Company Will Experience With Empowered Employees

- Far less turnover because employees feel as though they are important to the company

- Companies that empower their employees are more profitable

- Companies that empower their employees have a bigger talent pool to select from and promote from within more often than companies that have a traditional management structure.

- Happier clients because decisions can be made faster

- Here is a story about an empowered team that exemplifies the benefits your company will experience if presented with a few options:

Tea Kettles, A Newly Married Manager, An Aggressive Quota and an Empowered TEAM

Nadine is the sales manager for a tea kettle manufacturer. She manages a department that sells about $5 million annually. Her job is to manage the 5 sales people on staff at Teaworks, a manufacturer of tea kettles and tea accessories. Teaworks has independent distributors all over the country, in addition to servicing clients at some of the big box stores like Target, Macys, Lord & Taylor and Kohls. Sales are brisk and each of the 5 sales people has a booming client roster. Teaworks is very happy with Nadine. So happy in fact, at her annual review, they raise her quota to $6 million next year, citing their strong belief in Nadine's capabilities and her track record of always reaching her goals.

Nadine, recently married, met her husband at a conference 3 years ago and fell immediately in love with Don. They both rose to the top of their departments within their companies, Donald in customer service and Nadine in sales. They are in different industries, but the yearly conference on Customer Experience was a way for both Nadine and Donald to recharge their batteries, get new ideas to take to their teams, invigorate their creative sides and go back home ready to implement some of their findings within their respective departments. They share a lot of stories on sales, service, wins and losses over dinner.

While cooking his favorite chicken dish, with summer squash and sweet potato, Don asked Nadine about her day.

"I'm really in for it now," Nadine said. "My boss just raised my quota twenty percent! How am I ever going to make that happen? My phone rings off the hook now with my sales team needing price approvals, contract authorization, shipping advice. You know the drill. It all comes down to me. I've got some great sales people onboard, but management has us locked in tight on pricing, terms and contract exceptions. What am I going to do? I tell you what I should do, I should tell my boss the quota is just too aggressive."

Don poured a glass of chardonnay for Nadine and one for himself. He knew this was going to be a long night. Don is always concerned about Nadine, she takes everything so personally. Don listened intently as Nadine emptied her brain of all of the ways she could manage her schedule differently, adjust her gym schedule to allow for extra time at the office to make up for the extra work that was about to hit her. Twenty percent higher quota was going to mean at least another 5-10 hours a week in the office. When Scott raised Nadine's quota last year by just five percent, she was working several hours more a week and she was afraid her salespeople were going to hit the roof.

Don offered some great advice that night over chicken, chardonnay and coffee. "Why don't you get your team together first thing in the morning and talk it through with them. When I get stuck on a project or can't quite think something through properly, I involve my entire team. Ultimately, there is a solution to your quota increase. And the solution will be something acceptable to management I am sure. You have a loyal team, Nadine. We've had dinner with them, laughed with them and enjoyed their company on and off the clock. They will have your solution. Don't go changing your gym and work schedule just yet, Nay, I have faith they have an answer you will like."

Morning came and Nadine called an all-hands meeting at 8:30 a.m. David, who worked remotely, was called on the conference room phone and the other 4 sales people came in and sat down, three of the four with coffee, and the fourth with a Diet Coke. Nadine stopped at a local bagel shop for a dozen bagels hot out of the oven.

"Thanks for being here, everyone, and thanks, David, for joining us remotely. Let's get down to business, I know you all have packed schedules today, as I do as well. Scott has given us all an aggressive quota increase of twenty percent." Nadine paused, she could hear the groans of displeasure and see them all rolling their eyes, except David via remote, but she could only imagine his concern since he had Teawork's busiest territory including the Target and Kohls accounts. "Now I know we normally cover quotas and sales numbers individually, and I am happy to go through specifics with each of you, but as a team I am looking for some suggestions on how to handle this monster rise in our bottom line numbers."

Lots of ideas were discussed in that meeting, traveling to visit the top clients to improve service and customer experience, hiring an additional sales person to handle some of the lower-end merchandise and train them as a junior salesperson. Eve, the Diet Coke drinker in the meeting, made a suggestion about hiring an assistant to work with the sales team. "An assistant could help us with admin, shipping orders, and respond to some of our client questions via email." They even talked about a plan to work on the weekends to catch up on more administrative work so they could be in front of the client more during normal business hours.

None of these ideas were acceptable to the entire group until David proposed a program involving empowerment. "I have a client," David said, "That has a sales team about as big as ours. Here is what they do with their people. They give their sales people power to make pricing changes, shipping exceptions, contract revisions, service resolutions and delivery changes without the need to consult management." David paused long enough for Eve in the conference room to say, "I think David got disconnected. Either that or someone in upper management had him eliminated for coming up with that idea." The room erupted in laughter, and all but Nadine dismissed the idea as something management would never go for.

Nadine spoke up. "Tell me their story, David, how is this process working for them?" Knowing he had the spotlight, David chose his words carefully. "They have a sales team that has the ability to make decisions without the frequent interruptions of checking with management each time an exception or problem arises. They are similar to us in one respect, we both have awesome players in place." Nadine smiled, she worked many years assembling this hardworking, dedicated group of people. David continued, "But they work far less hours than we do, make a few more bucks and none of them seem to be tied down by so many memos and rules as we do." Nadine spoke up, "So are they interviewing?" Again the group broke out into laughter.

The meeting continued for about twenty minutes and Nadine had them all out the door by 9 a.m. and back at their desks working hard on the days inquiries and plans. Her promise to the team was that she would review with her management team and get back to them in the next few days with a solid plan. Later that night as Nadine prepped dinner, burgers and a baked potato, she told Don of David's idea. He loved it and just hoped that management loved it as well since he knew that her boss was fairly conservative. But he also knew her boss trusted Nadine, she was a loyal employee and always gave her job one hundred percent.

Within 48 hours, Nadine found herself in front of her boss, Scott, describing the meeting two days earlier with her sales team. She talked about the ideas David and the entire group came up with and was very happy when her boss asked, "What do you think Nadine? Do you feel as though this would work for your people?" Nadine reflected for a moment, remembering a few of the amazing highlights and victories her team had collected—David calling her to tell her about his closing the Target deal three years ago and how he had to take the red eye back from Minneapolis, so he wouldn't miss his son's first soccer game. Eve slept at the office one night because she was helping the shipping department box up a custom order for a special client she has. She knew this was the right team for this plan.

"I think they can do it, Scott, but we need to give them guidelines, expectations and time to make it come together. If we start with a base of understanding and let them know that we want them to think on their own, think creatively and outside the box, I really know my people will come through. We're invested in them and they want to do a good job for us. Empowering them to negotiate contracts without checking with me for every exception is a winning idea. I've checked out several companies that have a plan in place similar to the one we are considering here. Companies that empower their people have happier customers, a higher profit margin, close a greater percentage of deals, have increased productivity, have a higher employee satisfaction rating and hold on to their employees longer." She paused long enough for Scott to chime in. "Sounds like you are into this idea, Nadine. You've sold me. Now, let's make it happen and get to our quota."

Nadine pulled the group together later that day at 4:30. She talked about her conversation with Scott and presented a preliminary plan to get started. "Any pricing exceptions or negotiations are all yours to handle up to $5,000. Shipping exceptions and methods of delivery are yours to decide as well. You know our busy months, and I will give you the guidelines for overnight and long distance shipping. You have a $1,000 cap on delivery exceptions." Nadine laid out the rest of the plan after a few days of meeting with her individual salespeople. She even took a flight to visit David to work on the empowerment plan since it was his brainchild. They decided to name the project TeaPower.

Six months into TeaPower, Teaworks sales were up well over 20 percent. Nadine, who tracked sales like a hawk for that period of time, discovered that there had been only a few exceptions on pricing. Shipping exceptions were minimal and an analysis of pricing, shipping and contract changes revealed that many of the decisions the empowered sales team made were identical or even better than the decisions that Nadine or Scott would have made anyway. That made Nadine extremely happy. When asked about why they felt like the sales numbers were up so dramatically after just six months, many of the salespeople said they felt more like an owner of Teaworks; they felt more proud to be representing something they had decision making power for and they loved that they could think and act creatively. David said to Nadine in a TeaPower phone meeting, "My day is spent doing what I love to do. Spending time with my customers and not trying to fill out contract exception requests and negotiating with management. I feel I am more important to Teaworks now, and I love that I have more time to sell."

One year into the TeaPower project and Teaworks sales are up 35 percent from last year. The majority of the change is attributed to TeaPower, and Scott knows it. In a follow-up meeting Scott and Nadine discussed giving the sales team more power to make decisions, raising the pricing exceptions to $10,000 and shipping exceptions to $5,000. "Our sales team is incredible, they have really knocked it out of the park, Nadine. Great idea this TeaPower is." In response, Nadine said, "I'd love to take credit, Scott, but we are all in this together. David came up with the idea, the team worked on the plan and we all came together to make TeaPower a success. I'm just happy to have my life in order and a ton of very happy clients."

Action Items

1. Write a moral to the TeaWorks story. How do you see this fitting into your life?

2. List the ways in which empowering people within your organization will be helpful.

3. List the people within your organization or "inner-circle" that you would like to empower, and your expectations for those people.

CHAPTER 8

NICE GUYS ARE LEADERS

A leader is one who knows the way, goes the way
and shows the way.

~John Maxwell

Leadership comes in many shapes and sizes but one thing is certain; people are not born into a position of leadership. Birthright might give you a position of authority, but don't confuse the two—leadership and authority. A position of authority can be given to you, but you will need to *earn* leadership. Leaders do not live in ivory towers and are rarely behind the scenes barking orders. More often than not leaders are in the trenches and on the frontline. General George Patton said of leadership, "Do everything you ask of those you command." The nature of a leader is they want to be involved in every aspect of a project and plan of action because they ultimately take ownership of everything they are responsible for.

Leaders do not delegate all responsibility, they take on a good portion of the responsibility themselves. Stephen Covey is noted as saying, "Without involvement, there is no commitment. Mark it down, asterisk it, circle it, underline it. No involvement, no commitment."

And leaders know how to assemble a good team. People who follow the leader do so because they want to, not because they have to.

I've spent years studying and learning about leaders in many fields including technology, science, manufacturing and other fields, and I developed a series of myths about leadership. In addition there are many traits that leaders possess, and one that must be present. I will later discuss the one trait that I feel leaders must possess. For now, here are 5 myths that I have personally observed over the course of my career.

5 Leadership Myths

Leaders are born leaders.

Not true, anyone can become a leader. It will require effort, persistence, a positive attitude, lots of elbow grease and hands-on action. Leaders are put into a position of leadership by people who believe in them, would follow them to the end and who love them not because of a project, but because they love the person. Normal, everyday people become leaders because they earn the position. They have a tireless work ethic and are not afraid to roll up their sleeves and get dirty to get a job done. An important factor in becoming a leader also involves taking a certain risk, but if the risk doesn't pay off, a leader will admit he is wrong and take the blame. A true leader also understands the importance of building other leaders. True leaders create leadership in others.

Leaders are fearless.

Totally not true. Leaders have the same fears as you and me. Leaders have the ability to embrace their fears, have courage when confronted by their fears and stay the course in spite of their fears. Leaders are motivated by their fears, because in each fear there is hope to find a solution. Leaders are also passionate. They believe so much in what they are doing that the thought of not moving forward outweighs the fear of moving forward.

Goal setting and developing a plan of action are big fear crushers. Consider fear as a hurdle in the race to finish line. You may only have one fear, but often, you may have multiple fears like, "What if I fail," "I've never done this before, so I will look foolish," or "I can't do this." These fears are legitimate and moving beyond them will require action. Fear loves it when you are immobile. When you are moving forward and running the race, fear starts to subside. When you tackle one of your fears, the rest start to look smaller. The hurdles instead of getting higher, begin to get lower. The further into the race you get they can easily get stepped over. Now visualize the finish line, you won't even see that last fear. The granddaddy of them all, fear of failure, will disappear when you cross the finish line. A leader will help you run alongside those fears until they go away and help you over the hurdles that you find challenging to jump on your own.

Leadership is about power.

Incorrect. True leaders take responsibility and guide a group to make decisions as a team. Too many leaders are overly concerned about being in a position of power which could lead them to dictate to their followers. Oftentimes that will be met with a poor response from the group they believe they are leading. Leaders must help guide their group, get their vision to come into focus and assist in determining goals. They cannot effectively "tell" their group anything, but instead they need to "show" their group the way. Even if goals are not clear and vision is not laser focused, a leader must guide through the fog until the group's vision becomes clear. With the help of others in the group, a leader will guide a group on goal setting, strategy building and creating the framework for the specific project.

Computer and technology leader Michael Dell said, "You [leaders] have to show the way, even if you have no idea what to do." When you lead by example, people develop trust in you. Keep in mind as a leader, you are very dependent upon your followers. It's not the other way around. You need people to accomplish your goals, and without followers, you will not be able to move beyond square one.

Leaders are charming, full of personality and charismatic.

There are plenty of leaders that are far less than charming and delightful. Here are three traits that considerably outweigh charisma. One, leaders are effective communicators. They establish wonderfully productive relationships with people whom they come in contact. Two, great leaders have self-awareness, understand their shortcomings and develop a network of people who complement their weaknesses. Three, leaders have the ability to focus on a specific vision. They are excellent at goal setting and working on a plan of action. The enemy to action is inertia and complacency. Leaders are driven to move forward by nature, so they are always in a state of movement towards a goal.

Jim Collins, author of *Good to Great* and several other amazing books on business, says, "A charismatic leader is not an asset, it's a liability companies have to recover from. A company's long-term health requires a leader who can infuse the company with its own sense of purpose, instead of his or hers, and who can translate that purpose into action through mechanisms, not force of personality."

There is a specific style of leadership.

Myth! Leaders are chameleons. They can adjust their leadership style based upon the personalities of the people they are leading. If you spend a moment thinking about the diversity that exists within your own organization, you will understand the importance of many different leadership styles and approaches. A very popular personality assessment tool is called DiSC. The DiSC Model of Behavior was first proposed in 1928 by William Mouton Marston, a psychologist with a Ph.D. from Harvard. The DiSC Model is used as a tool to improve work productivity, teamwork and communication.

The "D" stands for Dominance. People scoring D are big picture people, blunt and to the point and accept challenges. The "I" stands for Influence. People scoring I are optimistic, are very enthusiastic, do not like to be ignored and like to work with others. "S" stands for Steadiness. S scorers are calm, supportive and don't like to be rushed. This type of person shows humility. Finally, "C" stands for Conscientiousness. The people scoring C like to work independently, want to know all of the details and fears being wrong. Leaders understand that there is a good chance that you will have 2 or more of the personality styles in their group. If they were to lead the same way regardless of who they are dealing with, they will be negatively viewed by their people. Great leaders understand the importance of changing leadership styles to get the most from a group and looks at his followers as individuals rather than en masse.

The one that can't get away—a leadership MUST.

Now that I have covered the myths of leadership, I'd like to spend time discussing the one trait that I feel must be present in all leaders. Without it, leadership will be short-lived.

If you had to pick just one quality that determined a leader, what would that quality be? Why do some people, no matter where they go in life, rise to become leaders of whatever organization they are a part of? Whether it be a Fortune 500 company, a nonprofit charity, a committee, a social circle or simply a pickup basketball team, these people seem to always have what it takes to lead. While there are many characteristics a leader has, there is one distinct quality that is critical, and without it, in my opinion, these people would not make the ultimate leadership cut.

I've read study after study, listened to lectures and speeches on leadership. I've read books about great leaders like Dale Carnegie, Napoleon Hill, Steve Jobs, Stephen Covey, Henry Ford and many others. And I have studied their systems, read articles about their lives, both professionally and personally, and I have found a common denominator in all true leaders.

Leaders sometimes have charisma, but not always. A leader might be strong-willed and dig their heels in to get a job done, but not always. And while persistence and tenacity are great leadership qualities, they are not requirements for being a leader. Leaders can be creative and, oftentimes people in a position of leadership think outside the box. But I have come across plenty of leaders in my career who work within rigid parameters and who are not very creative.

So what is the one quality that turns ordinary people into extraordinary leaders? True leaders show *gratitude*. True leaders understand the concept of honest appreciation and heartfelt praise. Leaders know the difference between "thank you" and "I appreciate you."

Leaders understand that nothing can be accomplished without support from others. Genuine gratitude and appreciation motivates others to want to pitch in and do a good job. We all want to be appreciated and it's proven, once we receive genuine appreciation, we will work harder to accomplish a task, project or responsibility.

Lots of research has been done on the effects of gratitude and appreciation in our lives. Gratitude gives us a feeling of elation and joy. Gratitude creates a human connection and helps us move towards even more collaborative relationships. Think about the connection you have with people you like the most. They are probably the people that appreciate you the most, show gratitude for a job well done, and sincerely regard your relationship and your efforts.

A side effect to showing gratitude is that it boosts the self-esteem of both the giver and the receiver, in addition to further strengthening the human connection. Showing gratitude is a true win-win for all parties involved. Leaders understand that gratitude is contagious. Once the gratitude-fest starts, your organization will never be the same.

Want to find the true leaders within your organization? Find the person that shows genuine gratitude and heartfelt appreciation and I will show you a team that is willing to follow her anywhere.

"People with everyday greatness are quick to exhibit everyday gratitude. They do not take life or the kindness of others for granted. They are eager to say thanks and the first to express praise. Many have found the best sleeping pill comes from counting one's blessings, naming them one by one."

~Stephen Covey

Action Items

1. List the goals you would set for the next 12 months if you had no possibility of failing.

2. List the traits that you exhibit as a leader, and also write down the areas that you need to work on to become a more effective leader.

3. Great leaders exhibit gratitude. I encourage you on a daily basis to find someone doing something right and tell them how much you appreciate them.

CHAPTER 9

NICE GUYS USE TEAMWORK TO MAKE A PLAN COMPLETE

No one can whistle a symphony. It takes an orchestra to play it.

~H.E. Luccock

I once overheard a manager at a local auto supply house saying to his staffer, "Teamwork makes the dream work." He was discussing the importance of a positive relationship between his staffer and the delivery person on staff at the store. On a daily basis, more than any other inspirational subject, I see quotes displayed on posters, sent in forwarded e-mails, posted on blogs and Tweeted on the topic of teamwork. I think that's partly because sports take such an upfront role in our society, and the idea of promoting teamwork naturally fits into this environment quite easily.

Here are several quotes that create a great visual for me and give me the feeling of being a part of something bigger:

"Individually we are one drop, together we are an ocean."

R. Satoro

"Good teams become great ones when the members trust each other enough to drop the 'me' for 'we'."

Phil Jackson

"Alone we can do so little, together we can do so much."

Helen Keller

"Teamwork is the fuel that allows common people to attain uncommon results."

Andrew Carnegie

No matter the discipline from which you come from, teamwork is an essential part of accomplishing goals. The task of writing a book does not solely consist of a writer sitting in a room and coming up with words on a screen. The process of writing a book involves editors, publishers, writing coaches, inspiration from others, cheerleaders and the guy sitting down writing his thoughts out. I could have never accomplished writing this book had it not been for all the others on my team.

Many of us forget that in order to get most projects complete, most tasks done and to accomplish anything worthwhile, we can't do it alone. It does take a village to make it all happen. And while cheerleaders are extremely important to help motivate us and keep us moving in the right direction, nothing can compare to another set of boots on the ground helping to get a task complete.

Some teams are formal—sports teams, project teams and management teams. But there are also an entire series of teams we may not actually view as a team, but rather as a group of people that must work as a team because they have a common cause. For example, when you check into a hotel, everyone from the valet that takes your car, the front desk person, the housekeeper, the service staff at the coffee shop and the security staff that watches the garage overnight. They are all a part of a team that must carry a common mission. And that mission is to make sure you have a great experience at the hotel. Hotels big and small that operate as a cohesive unit with a central vision, unified departmental goals and a common concern for the customer will be the most successful regardless of the rates they charge or the profits they make. Conversely, if the accounting department has a goal only focused on saving the hotel money and cutting corners, and the housekeeping department focuses just on getting rooms empty earlier so they can get their job done quickly, and the valet cuts staff to save the department budget on overtime, who ultimately is the one that will suffer? The customer.

Instead, a team of valued and empowered employees working on improving the customer experience with an eye on the bottom line and saving the parent company money will ultimately lead to a company that is profitable AND cares about their customers. Happy customers equal more overnight stays. The team wins, the customer wins and everyone is happy.

I presented my Nice Guys Finish First program to the staff of the luxury hotel brand in Washington, D.C. Prior to being given the stage, the general manager of the hotel was going through a series of awards and announcements. As a part of one of the awards presented, he had a financial award given to the department with the best hotel money saving suggestion. The qualifier was that the suggestion could in no way diminish the quality of the guest experience and extra focus was given if the suggestion actually improved the guest experience. The winning suggestion involved taking some of the convenience items out of the shower and placing them on the countertop instead, so that when the shower was turned on, the packaging was not compromised and could be used again if the guest did not use the items on day one.

After the meeting, in discussing how they came up with this idea, the department head told me the entire department sat down in the conference room (not on company time) and placed all of the items they use, in the course of carrying out their responsibilities, on the conference room table. While someone took notes and listed all of the items on a whiteboard they determined as a team what items could be taken off the table. For example, using lower quality sheets to save money would adversely affect the customer experience, so that item could not be used. Eliminating the robes and slippers from the closest was also taken out of the running, because although only used a small percentage of the time, any reduction in the quality of the guest experience would equal a fail. When all was said and done, they were left with two potential money saving ideas. First, they would save time (which equates to dollars) by eliminating the decorative folding of their towels. I'm confident you have seen these towel fold creatures if you have ever gone on a cruise. The winning idea of placing the convenience items in a better spot was a better idea to the department because one of the housekeepers remembered the smile on young guest's face when she first saw the towel fold elephant housekeeping created. The housekeeper rallied and explained that by eliminating the time would be great for money savings, but the memories created by an 8-year-old will last a lifetime. Teamwork at its finest.

Another example is when I worked in the mortgage business, I was a part of a huge team. I recall it took the efforts of many people to get a new home buyer from mortgage application to settlement day. The team consisted of the loan officer, the processing agent, the underwriter, the real estate agent, the home inspector, the title agent and all of their support staff as well, just to name a few. You may only interact with a few of these people throughout the process of buying a home, and yet the entire team is responsible for getting you into your new digs.

There are a variety of players on a team. Each player on a team is unique with their own set of personality traits. Not surprisingly, certain team members naturally rise to the rank of leader, while others situate themselves as worker bee, minutes taker, organizer, supporter and several other positions within the group. There are thinkers, doers, analyzers, experts and others that will be on your team, involved in your project and a part of the plans. Your job will be to get along with all of them while completing the task assigned to the team. Below are series of things that you should learn to become proficient with while not losing site that you have a goal as a team.

Learn to delegate. As a part of a team, learning how to delegate is essential. Only tackle the tasks that you feel competent in completing. Remember, the rest of the team is counting on you to finish the responsibilities you are given. This is not a time to swallow hard and take on too much, but it is a time to deal with the task you have been given. When dividing up the "tasks" needed to complete a project, speak up when you feel as though you have an area that you consider yourself to have a certain level of expertise.

Become an effective communicator. In order to work closely with others on your team you need to learn to open your mouth and talk.

But more important than talking, you need to learn when to keep your mouth closed as well. I had a teacher in high school that always said, "Sandler, you have two ears and one mouth, use them proportionally." I also had a music teacher that always said to the class, "People, be sure brain is engaged before putting mouth in gear." A great teammate facilitates conversation, but understands when it is important to stop having meetings and start taking action. Remember, it's the goal of the team to get stuff done, not to chitchat.

Take the WE philosophy and drop out of the I-zone. As a society, we are so concerned with ourselves as individuals. Many of us get so focused on the "I" that we have trouble when we are put on a team. Getting out of the I-zone and into the We-zone is one of the first characteristics that employers look for when interviewing others for a job. The ability to get along with others.

Life is about compromise. Being on a team requires understanding the importance of give and take. Compromise is truly an art form on a team because all parties need to feel as though they have given up little and won a lot. Relationships require work, and if handled correctly all players on the team will come walk away from a project closer to one another and happier.

Everyone gets a chance to play in the game and be the MVP. Your time to take the ball and run to the basket is not now. The philosophy should be that everyone is a star at some point during a project involving your team. If your team works together permanently and you are not just dealing with a short term project, the attitude and your actions are a part of your team's overall culture.

Give credit to one and all. A win for one is a win for all. Being quick to pass praise, to be humble and to point the spotlight on others on the team is a noble trait. It's a tough skill to master, but you will be amazed at the amount of people that will want to be on your team, in your department or to work near you when you become a credit giver. The best way to deliver credit is to do it publicly and in front of the entire team. Providing credit directly to the worthy individual is great, but take it to the next level and offer praise in front of the entire group. It's important, however, that you don't overdo it. Since the team's goal is to work together, praise the entire group as well in the process. Saying something like, "The entire team has done an excellent job at helping save money on this project. Joan has been such a valuable team member for adding some of her amazing ideas to help us reach our goals as well. Thanks, everyone, for your work and thanks, Joan, for digging deep and helping us get there as well." Another great way to provide credit is in writing. A handwritten thank you note is a great personal touch to say thanks. Best of all, it does not need to be sent from the team leader. If your position on the team is not as leader, a thank you note is still completely acceptable as a form of showing gratitude. A handwritten note says several things, but most importantly it says that you care about the recipient, you respect the recipient, and you are genuinely thankful.

Be slow to criticize. No one likes a critic that criticizes for the sake of pointing out faults. Diplomacy and constructive criticism is good if new ideas develop and you present your ideas properly. Just as giving credit will earn you points and make you popular, becoming a critic will drive people away from you. Want a sure fire way be the last one picked on a team or your ideas to be silenced? Criticize quickly and you will be that guy. I can specifically remember having a conversation with my daughter Rachel when she returned home from her first day in third grade. I asked what her favorite part of this special day was for her. Rachel said, "My favorite part of the day was recess, because I went out to the playground and made sure everyone was following all the rules." That maybe ok for a 9-year-old, but it isn't a good plan for an adult. On occasion, it's ok not to follow all the rules, and it's ok not to point out everyone's faults. The vast majority of the time, your team will follow the rules, but there will be some instances where bending the rules to accommodate a situation will be acceptable. Thinking outside the box will lead to creativity and fresh ideas; in those cases you will feel your team really come together.

Let empathy be your guide. Put yourself in a position to understand things from your teammate's perspective. We all have a habit of getting so caught up in our own set of responsibilities, problem solving and agenda that we forget that everyone else has their own responsibilities, problems and agenda as well. Try your best to get into your teammates' mindsets. A situation that may seem easily dealt with for you, may be problem of Mount Everest proportion to others. Here is your opportunity to forge a great relationship. People become closer to people that help them resolve issues. But people build extraordinary relationships when they are simply listened to. Be present during any conversation involving your teammate's problems and determine whether he is looking for you to be a good listener versus a good problem solver. As a male, I sometimes forget that oftentimes women that are teammates don't always look to have their problems solved. Rather, they just want to be heard, hugged and know that someone cares, and that someone is listening and being empathetic towards their situation. Work hard at empathy, it is key to building relationships and being a valuable team member.

Understand team goals versus personal goals. Is it your destiny to be a senior vice president? Or are you looking for a 3 day work week? Are you trying to put a kid through college and need the job for the extra family income or the benefits? Sometimes we have no idea why people do what they do. Do you know the best way to determine what motivates your team? Ask them! Prior to getting underway on a project or task or at some point during the initial stages of having a team come together, as a team, discuss the goals of the team. On a white board (we used to call them chalk boards when I was early in my career) draw a line down the middle of the board. On the left side list all the team goals. On the right side, list the individual goals of your teammates. You may discover things like recognition, reward, advancement and appreciation are goals on the right side of the list. And it's ok for the individual goals to be achieved, as long as the team goal is achieved in the process as well.

Learn to say NO. I saved this one for last because most people reading this book are fundamentally NICE, but we all have some challenges with saying no. People oftentimes have a fear of saying no because they might feel saying no is rude or mean, could potentially cause a conflict or argument or they just want to be agreeable. The problem with never saying no is that you will find that if you don't learn to say no, you will be the chef, prep cook and dishwasher for your entire group. Saying no while providing an explanation will show your group you are conscious of your time management, your area of expertise and your capabilities as well. If your schedule is packed tight and you accept another timely task assigned to your team, you may not have the ability to finish the task in time, thereby holding your entire team back. Learn that saying no is ok and a part of life. People will appreciate your honesty when you say, "Thanks for thinking of me for this, but it really isn't the best fit for what I am capable of." Or if time management is an issue, you can say something like, "I'd really love to take this task but I want to be fair to the team and give it the proper time needed. Right now is not a good time for me to take on this responsibility." Practice saying no. If needed, practice it in front of a mirror. Smile, breathe and be genuine. Your teammates will forgive you for saying no, I promise.

Being a part of team is extremely satisfying. Nothing can compare to the elation felt when a team collectively achieves a goal, wins a victory or successfully completes a project.

Brian Tracy, author, business consultant and speaker, says of teamwork. "Teamwork is so important that it is virtually impossible for you to reach the heights of your capabilities or make the money that you want without becoming very good at it." I couldn't agree more.

Action Items

1. List the characteristics of a good team player. Have others on your team do the same and discuss those characteristics with others on the team.

2. Write down 3 teams that you are a part of professionally and 3 teams that you are a part of personally. What ways do you feel you could improve as a part of the team? For example, could you do a better job communicating with your team? Could you be more effective at following up with team members?

3. Learn to celebrate small successes on your team. Make sure you celebrate the small victories. Write down short term celebrations and stick to the plan. If your team achieves a goal, make sure you take time to celebrate.

CHAPTER 10

NICE GUYS CREATE AN ENVIRONMENT OF HAPPINESS

Success is not the key to happiness. Happiness is the key to success. If you love what you are doing, you will be successful.

~Albert Schweitzer

I've spent my entire life being happy. Even when things were challenging in my life, the temporary facade of not-so-happy thoughts, sadness, pain, heartache or failure has always been wiped away by my happiness.

I can trace it all back to when I was young. As a child, my mom would always figure out a way to make a bad situation good or a good situation even better. As a single parent, my mom raised my brother and me in a small apartment in Baltimore. I remember always laughing and being happy in that little apartment. My brother, David, and I shared a bedroom and we got along very well. I always looked up to and admired David. He was a great athlete, had a nice stable of friends and seemed to always be heading places. And although I know he acted like he didn't want me to tag along when he joined his friends, deep down I knew he was ok with it. At least that's what my mom always said. We had a good life.

I believe life is all about having a positive attitude and a great outlook on life. With happiness as a sidekick, I think anything is possible. Happiness is an attitude; happiness is truth. I challenge anyone to try and be happy and to be dishonest. Even as a child I always aligned myself with people that were happy, content and very positive.

There is lot of interesting research on why some people are happy while others gravitate towards dark cloud thinking and negative attitudes. Many factors determine happiness, but there is one thing that researchers have determined with certainty. Money cannot buy happiness. Studying lottery winners validates this theory. A study of multi-million dollar state lottery winners, when asked just after picking the winning tickets, the winners expected their life to change dramatically. What was discovered was that happiness among the winners temporarily improved, but it was only for a short-term period. In the long-term a pattern of "same old" problems, issues and concerns crept back into their lives.

So if it is not money that makes people happy over the long run, what is it that can keep someone seeing smiley face yellow throughout their lives? Here is a list of important factors to help you reach your happiness quota:

Happy people show gratitude.

What's the use in being happy unless you share your happiness with others by showing gratitude? Express your feeling of gratitude and thankfulness to a coworker that helped you on a project. Give your brother a call just to tell him you love him. Thank your boss for providing you a bit of extra time to get your work done. Most of all, be sincere about your gratitude, cherish the fact that others are taking their time, energy and resources to help you. Expressing gratitude will make you feel good about *you*. If you don't believe me, I challenge you to pick up the phone right now and call a family member to say thank you for all the support and guidance they have provided through the years. I promise you it will make you feel amazing.

Happy people are not focused on the prize alone.

I have planned many vacations in my life and while going on vacation creates its own level of happiness, there is plenty of excitement from the planning vacation as well. I can remember the beach trips we took when I was a young boy. Because my mom didn't have a lot of money, we would often go to the beach just for the day, driving 3 hours in each direction to get to our sun drenched destination. While the trip was fun in the sun, I can remember the anticipation weeks ahead of time, talking to my brother about playing frisbee on the sand, riding waves on our rafts, playing miniature golf.

Think about this example for a moment. Gift cards are the gift that keep on giving. When you get a gift card as a present you are being given two gifts in one. First, receiving the card creates a feeling of happiness. Your mind starts to walk the through the dozens of goodies that you might want to purchase at the store. Second, when you actually go to the store or make your purchase online, there is a certain magic to using the card as well. When in doubt of what gift to buy for me, a gift card is always a great choice. You are sure to double the pleasure of the recipient. Some people might claim gift cards are impersonal. I say, "No way!" They are the gift that keeps giving.

Happy people work hard.

A challenging job, done well, has a level of satisfaction that cannot be achieved if you are given a reward for no reason at all. Happy people set their sights on a reward, work hard to achieve their goals and take time to celebrate their victories. Research shows that people that work hard tend to be happier. Happier people build better relationships and also achieve their goals more often.

When I was 13 I took on my first job at a place called Geoffrey's Ski Hut. The store was in the heart of my hometown of Pikesville, MD. Geoffrey, a neighbor at the time, would drive me into work with him. The shop sold skis and winter fashion. In the off-season, all the stock for the upcoming winter was shipped to the shop. Even as a positive and happy 13-year-old kid I was not happy with the sight of seeing hundreds of pairs of skis that were in need of being prepped for the season. I refocused my "vision" of the skis, and instead of seeing hours and days of work ahead of me, I thought about all of the happy people that would be heading to a snowy destination. Mentally, each pair I opened, I named another 13-year-old kid, just like me, who would be enjoying the slopes. The work was hard, tedious and repetitious, but it helped me understand the importance of working toward a goal while at the same time, remaining happy with my work.

Happy people love what they do, and do what they love.

If you love what you do, you will be happy. In 1980, I worked my way through my junior and senior years of high school. As a 16-year-old, I was excited with the opportunity to make money and to be independent. Independence was always my goal. Money made it possible for me to own my own car, buy the clothes I wanted to buy and enjoy the things important to a 16-year-old: putting gas in my car, buying video games, eating at McDonald's and buying Guess jeans.

I worked at a place called The Great Cookie. My coworker Fred Wachter and I developed a sales system that was second to none. Early on, working at The Great Cookie we discovered that people don't buy cookies because they are hungry. People buy cookies because it makes them happy. The happier they are, the more cookies they buy. If we made our customers laugh, they would buy more cookies.

The weekends at The Great Cookie were always packed. We would have a line of 5 or 6 people deep. Fred and I had a routine, we would joke around with each other, get into pretend arguments, involve the customers in our interaction and sell, sell, sell. Our boss wanted nothing to do with our plan, however. Jeff wanted us to shut up and do our job. But Fred and I knew, joking around and selling cookies WAS our job. And our sales proved it.

The foundation of being happy at work was established, and I vowed to create a level of happiness no matter what job I was doing. I maintained a handful of jobs prior to going to college and I was true to my word. I always had a job that put me in front of the public. My love for being a people pleaser created a great work ethic for me. My positive attitude paved the way for me to land every job I applied for, and although I wasn't always the highest qualified applicant, I always got a call back.

Since that job at The Great Cookie, I have learned many valuable lessons about happiness in the work place. Decades later, as the owner of an entertainment company, I conduct interviews for applicants looking to be a DJ or technical staffer for my company. As I conduct the interview, I talk about the importance of having a positive attitude, being happy and being dependable. There is a pattern happy people follow. My discovery is that happy people are dependable people, arrive early for appointments, and speak positively of others. Negative people are excuse makers, often late for commitments and are not very positive about the future.

Happy people have goals and a purpose.

Goals, direction and finding a meaning in life are extremely important when growing business and growing relationships. Happy people are goal setters. They have a plan and they work hard. Happy people are not afraid to fail because they have a very positive attitude and outlook on life. They understand that failing is a part of the success process. Their self-esteem is intact and they take constructive criticism very well. Criticism has seeds of truth, so a happy person shapes future decisions on the truths. Criticism builds character and humility, and helps them to make better future decisions because they have focus on the future. Much more about goal setting in an upcoming chapter, but know that happy people are goal setting animals, visualize the future and see that they have a purpose for that future.

Happy people are optimistic

The glass is always half full when you are happy. Lost a job? Not a problem for happy people, they will be optimistic and look for an even better one. Just broke up with their boyfriend or girlfriend? There is plenty of fish in the sea. Happy people are always setting themselves up for something fabulous and putting themselves in a situation to win. It's not the situations that life throws at you, but how you handle them that counts. While some people focus on the negative that life throws at them, a happy person realizes that they must not get caught in the rut of doom and gloom. Early in my career I lived in New Jersey working for a company called The Professional Resume and Writing Service. It was my first real job out of college and I was excited to interview for it. I interviewed well, landed a management position and was excited to begin making my own way in life as a recent college graduate. I quickly advanced with the company and loved my responsibilities. Part of my sales management job was to visit each office in my territory weekly and collect the checks and cash received by each of 8 offices in the region.

I decided at the end of one of the collection days I would visit my friend Richard in New York. After visiting with Richard I went to get back into my car. It was gone, and so were all of the checks, cash and paperwork stashed in the trunk. Stolen. I was devastated. To add insult to injury, I did not have a very compassionate boss, and within a few days, it was obvious to me I was not going to get much support from them to try and recover my vehicle or the cash and checks that were in my car. I ended up quitting the job since they were so unsupportive.

When I left the job, I immediately went to work trying to find another job. I quickly found a job in northern New Jersey working for a company called Medix, Blue Cross and Blue Shield. In the process of finding the job, I developed a network of friends and colleagues, several of which I still have today, over 30 years later. Had it not been for my stolen car, I may not have developed the great circle of friends that helped get me to my next position. Although, at the time, I was not very happy, I dug in my heels and got to work, networking and developing opportunities for myself. Happy people are always optimistic and make the best out of every situation.

Happy people have happy friends.

You can tell a lot about a person by the company they keep. Happy people tend to associate with other happy people. Since happy people like to focus on the positive side of a situation, they remain very positive. Since they like to remain happy, they foster positive and healthy relationships. When something negative happens in a happy person's life, they work out of the situation quickly with the support of other happy people. Have you ever noticed that when people who are negative have something bad happen, they immediately go into a downward spiral of negative thoughts, conversations, and actions? Somehow, the negative situation was probably caused by a conspiracy, or so they think. Conversely, positive happy people lend a supportive shoulder to lean on, help others overcome the adversity, act as a cheerleader and move on with life. Problem solved.

One additional reason happy people hang out with other happy people is because they really do live by the Golden Rule. They treat others as they would like to be treated. Happy people embrace that principle because they are caring, kind and compassionate and they want to have others around them that feel the same way.

Happy people work through the blues.

Have you ever noticed that when people who are negative have something bad happen, they immediately go into a downward spiral of negative thoughts, conversations, and actions? While happy people generally live a happy life, sometimes it's challenging to be happy 24 hours a day 7 days a week. Happy people work through the challenges with an attitude of negativity by acting happy. Doing small acts of kindness for themselves or for others will often do the trick. It's surprising if you do positive things when you are feeling "low" how effective it can be in bringing you back to positive. The worst thing you could do for yourself is get caught in the rut of "stinkin' thinkin." A very easy way to help yourself out of the blues is to look back to all of the positive you have created in life. Keep a file of positive client comments, love notes from your significant other, photographs from fun family vacations or trips you have taken. You can quickly bring yourself back to happy by taking these simple actions.

I am sure there are many more factors to creating and maintaining happiness. These are the most consistent factors that I have observed over the decades of building my businesses. But one factor remains highest on my list. And that is that successful people are happy people. Because happy people work hard at maintaining happiness, they wear their happiness as a badge of honor. I welcome happy people into my life because I believe in my heart they make the world a better place to live.

Action Items

1. List 5 factors you feel would help you have a happy life. What are you doing today to help you with these factors?

2. Pick up the phone or tell someone close to you right now that you appreciate them in your life. A great way to put yourself in a happy place is to create your own "happy bubble." Catching someone doing something right or telling someone you appreciate them will boost your happiness instantly. Don't believe me, go ahead and give it a try.

3. The next time you find yourself in a "rough spot" and negativity enters your life, surround yourself with as much positive as you can. Although it's natural to wallow in your negativity, do your best to work through it quickly. List 3 people who can help you out of that rough spot. Call upon them to help you get back to happy.

CHAPTER 11

NICE GUYS HAVE POSITIVE ATTITUDES

The only disability in life is a bad attitude.

~Scott Hamilton

I am confident that prior to picking up my book you already understood the importance of a positive attitude, both professionally and personally. A positive attitude will help you win out on a job interview if all else is equal. A positive attitude will allow you to face challenging obstacles in your life and help you move through them. If you get in a fender bender or have a disagreement with a coworker, a properly aligned attitude can make all the difference. What you may not realize is the extent to which a positive attitude will propel you forward in life.

A positive attitude is a great partner to many other traits as well. A positive attitude coupled with a sense of humor can turn just about any situation into a win. A positive attitude and tenacity will allow you to coast through the most trying times. Want a sure fire way to remain positive when something negative happens to you? Laugh out loud, then do it again. Laughing is a great release of negative energy and will let you open to welcome the positive in. If you are pulling a late night at the office because a project is due before you go on vacation and you are missing your kid's ballgame, a positive attitude will help get you in the right frame of mind. Look at it this way, the project is helping you in your position at work, and thereby allowing you the freedom of enjoying a nice relaxing getaway with your entire family.

There is a rule when it comes to attitudes and it's an easy one to remember. Rule: You get to pick your attitude. You are 100% in control, and your attitude is up to you. So the question may not be why you should have a positive attitude, because you know it's always better to have a positive attitude, but instead HOW can you create and maintain a positive attitude. We discussed in the chapter "A Pattern for Success" the importance of consistency as a part of the success process. Having a positive attitude, similar to other success principles must be applied consistently over a long period of time to have a favorable long term result.

So how is it that you are able to pick your attitude when the world sometimes seems to be working against you and you're struggling? Follow my logic for a moment. When the times are challenging, and times *will* get challenging, that is the best time to pick a positive attitude. Sure, it is easy to be happy and up and positive when times are good. But make it a habit to work hard at remaining positive through the bad times too. With a positive attitude you are likely to be winning much more often. And life is about winning.

There are a few tricks and tactics you will need to use to help yourself get in a positive frame of mind. Here comes the HOW part. You must consistently speak to yourself (self-talk) in a positive manner. We are our own worst critics. If you said to someone else the things that you say to yourself, you'd be walking around with a black eye more times than not. Stop the negative talk, it's not good for you mentally and it's bringing you down. Negative self-talk is like a snowball, the more you talk down to yourself the worse your attitude gets. As your attitude gets progressively worse, your bad mood amplifies. Also, you are creating a negative environment around you, making everyone else miserable as well. Being your own worst critic is a big challenge to overcome. But using positive self-talk is your ticket out of Gloomyville. Stop the negative self-talk and put yourself on the fast pass to Happy Town. Try these positive words: "I am worthy," "I will succeed," "I see myself happy," "I can do this," and "I have confidence." Erase these negative words: "I can't do it," "I won't be able to," "I've never done that before," and "I'm going to fail if I try."

The reason most people fail is not because they try and don't succeed. Most people fail because they never give themselves a chance to succeed. Speak it into existence and talk yourself into a positive place.

Next, get yourself moving. An object in motion stays in motion according to Newton's First Law. If you get yourself moving you are going to get out of the way of your problem. Your brain needs to be given a diversion and you getting involved in a project or conversation or activity will help to get you away from the blues and bad attitude previously created.

As a DJ for over 25 years I noticed something interesting about a dance floor filled with people. I discovered that getting people up from their table to begin dancing is much more difficult than getting them to stay on the dance floor once they start dancing. People look for the perfect song to spark their involvement and begin dancing. However, if they are on the floor, they would dance to almost anything as long as there is a beat. Your brain works the same way when it comes to attitude. If you are feeling a dose of negativity, don't stay still, get your brain moving in a positive direction. You will quickly find you can get yourself out of the slump if you simply get it moving. And it will keep moving in a positive direction if you keep the positive energy grooving.

Finally, think like a winner and be an optimist. Winners are always looking for the silver lining. My dad used to tell a funny story about a young man locked in a room with nothing more than horse manure. The room smelled horrible and when put in the room the young man initially was not happy. To further make it a bad scene, the door was locked. About an hour later the door was unlocked and all that could be seen was the young man diving into the horse manure. With each dive into the waste his smile got bigger and bigger. When asked why he was so happy the young man said, "With all this poop in here, there has got to be a pony too!" Be an optimist, see the pony and not the poop.

When your mind starts to open up to all the great possibilities, you begin to notice more and more positivity. You will start to experience a funnel of positive feelings beginning with one feeling and opening up to a whole host of positive feelings. Your brain cannot be both negative and positive at the same time. Your positive, optimistic thoughts will overwhelm any dose of negativity you have and even big problems will evaporate the further you climb up the funnel.

There are additional benefits to maintaining a positive attitude. It's proven, being positive will reduce your stress level. The less stress you have in your life the more positive you will be. Win-win. Reduced stress will also create an environment where you can think clearly and be more focused on your goals. People that are stressed tend to have more anxiety, troubles and crisis in their lives. Talk about a triple threat spiral of gloom. Scientific studies have proven that stress creates a weakened immune system. Add poor health into the equation and you are again looking at bad news for bad attitudes.

I am an extremely positive person, but I am also a realistic person. I do not expect every day of life to be positive. Also, I am not a rah-rah kind of guy. Rah-rah is temporary and usually last as long as it takes you to walk from your car to your front door. You are going to have some down days. My wish for you is to have a permanent fix if you have a negative attitude. Even Mr. Nice Guy, me, has days slightly offbeat and negative. However, those days will be few and far between when you start to work on the habits to move you to positive. The old you might have had a full day of negative thinking. The new you might only have a few hours of negative attitude. Eventually, with practice, a negative attitude will be able to be erased by giving yourself a few moments to talk yourself out of it. At that point, you will realize YOU choose your attitude, your emotion and your state of mind and no one is in control of you besides you; and that is truly when you start to win in life.

Now that I have covered some of the ways to eliminate negativity from your thinking, I want to spend a moment and discuss 2 key gateway problems that can lead to negative thinking and ultimately to a negative attitude. The first big precursor to negativity is worry. You need to know this if you don't already. Most worry is needless and will amount to nothing more than expended energy. As Kimberly "Sweet Brown" Wilkens said, "Ain't nobody got time for that!" And neither do you.

Dalai Lama said, "If a problem is fixable, if a situation is such that you can do something about it, then there is no need to worry. If it's not fixable, then there is no help in worrying. There is no benefit in worrying whatsoever." It may not be clear to you but you should spend some time reading that quote over and over again. No matter the situation, worry will accomplish absolutely nothing.

I can remember my transition from college to my first full-time job in the workplace. With the job came a big move from my hometown of Baltimore, Maryland to Cherry Hill, New Jersey. With the move came worry. I had dozens of worries. What if the job didn't work out? What if I lost my job? What if I couldn't pay my bills? What if I failed at managing the territory I have been assigned to? The worry and anxiety kept me up at night for many weeks prior to the move. I was so gripped by worry it affected every decision I was making prior to the move. And I was driving everyone around me crazy.

As I look back now, that move was one of the best decisions I ever made. It taught me independence and decision making. It helped me to become a better manager of people, taught me how to manage my money and budget properly. Many of the early lessons about life, business and relationships I learned as a result of my 5 years living in New Jersey. Had I let the worry immobilize me, I would have missed out on all of the great experiences I had by making the move.

The second problem that can create a negative results is fear. Fear is a paralyzer. It can stop you dead in your tracks if you let it. And the greatest fear of all is the fear of the unknown. People in general are fearful of change, and although a situation may be bad, the fear of the unknown is worse. Jack Heath said, "Better the devil you know than the devil you don't." I got myself through some tough situations by rationalizing with myself. The line I would say to myself again and again is, "What's the worst that can happen?" Those words have gotten me through many situations to date. If the answer to that question is a situation I can deal with, then I forge ahead and let fear fall to my side. Do not let fear and worry hold you back. Fear stands for False Evidence Appearing Real. There is no reason for it, so let it go.

Focus on getting rid of your worry and fear, and you will surely leave behind two key reasons for negative thinking and a negative attitude.

Author's note:

It has taken many years of working hard at maintaining a positive attitude to truly understand the importance of being positive about life in general. I've worked myself out of some bad situations over the years by maintaining a positive attitude. I had a father that was a great business person but not the best father in the world. But I was able to take away from the relationship what I needed and leave the rest behind. I've learned many lessons about what type of father I wanted to be to my kids, and I have learned what type of businessman I need to be in order to achieve success in business. Later in my life, I found myself in a marriage that could not be fixed and dealt with the pain of divorce. I had a choice of how I wanted to react to both of those challenging situations in my life, and I chose not to get stuck with worry, fear or a negative attitude about relationships as a result. When it's up to me, I choose to win, and not let a bad situation define me and cause me to make bad decisions about my future. Given a choice, and there is always a choice, I choose to have a positive attitude.

Action Items

1. Write down your mantra. Your mantra is something you are going to say to yourself to when your attitude is anything less than positive. Your mantra can be as simple as saying to yourself, "I am good, I am worthy of great things, I am positive about where my life is going."

2. Draw a picture of a goal that you would like to achieve. Keep it in a place you can see daily. I recently drew a picture (stick figures) of me in front of a large TED Talk audience. The small piece of paper is taped to my bathroom mirror. It's my daily reminder, in picture form, of a goal that I will achieve.

3. Set aside time every day to reaffirm that you are valuable and that you have an important place in this world. A positive attitude is rooted in your belief you are good, you are safe and you have a positive impact on those around you.

CHAPTER 12

FAILURE IS A PART OF SUCCESS

Don't be embarrassed by your failures, learn from them and start again.

~Richard Branson

You might be wondering why I would ever write a chapter about failure in a book about success. Writing a book about being productive, efficient, grateful, happy and successful should be about positive thoughts, energy and feelings, right? Absolutely, but I also want to be realistic. Odds are overwhelming that if you have achieved any level of success in life, you didn't just grab the brass ring on your first pass. I am fairly confident that you had some missteps along the way, as I have.

In 1991, just before going to work in the mortgage business, I had the idea of getting my real estate license and selling homes to generate an income. Although I passed the exam to get my license, I never accomplished selling even one house. I didn't like the entire process of entering listings into the computer, taking indecisive people around to look at homes, getting calls late at night by sellers. It wasn't for me, and the results proved it. Not one house sold, no commissions earned, and in my opinion at the time, this was a failure. Looking back though, had I not attempted to make the real estate business work out, I never would have developed a relationship with an old classmate from high school that was hitting it big in the mortgage business.

Brian Sacks, my boss in the mortgage business, was a great leader. He was the manager of our local office of First Town Mortgage. Brian was the most successful person my age I had ever met. He is motivated, talented, well liked and extremely positive. He taught me about goal setting, working through tough times, staying extremely positive and delivering award-winning service. Brian was funny too. He always used to have these great sayings. We would call each other "Seymore" (I have no idea why, but that's just what we called each other). Regarding great customer service, he'd say, "Seymore, in the kingdom of the blind, the one-eyed man is king." What he was saying was I didn't have to be perfect, but I needed to be better than the other guy. And he was right. We don't have to be perfect to be successful. We are allowed to fail, lose deals, mess up with paperwork and break the rules by accident. As long as you get up one more time than you get knocked down, everything is going to be all right. Each time I would have a setback, Brian was there to pick me up, help me learn from my mistake and shove me out the door again. He'd say, "Seymore, don't come back here until you sell something." I had great respect for Brian, and I listened to his wisdom and followed his advice.

I appreciated Brian's presence in my life at a time when I was only handful of years out of college and still very green when it came to business. Brian helped me earn Rookie of the Year status among the handful of offices that First Town operated, and for two years running helped me win trips to the Caribbean Islands because of my sales success.

Brian also taught me the importance of getting up after falling down. Although we were the same age, Brian was an old soul and the entire office would listen to his sage advice. If I ever had a down day or a lost sale or things weren't going just right, Brian would talk to me about some of the great teachers and influencers of the 1900s. Brian would quote famous businessmen and authors like Napolean Hill and Dale Carnegie.

One very important lesson to learn about failure. Learning to fail is a part of the success process. Great leaders have been great failures along the path to success. Prior to being elected president, Abraham Lincoln was defeated in a run for state legislature and Speaker of the House, failed to get nominated for Congress, was defeated in a bid for U.S. Senate, failed to get nominated for Vice President, and failed in business. Talk about someone who worked through failure before being elected to the highest position in U.S. government.

Steve Jobs, arguably one of the most dominant and influential people of the digital age flunked out of college and was fired from the company he founded. In addition, Jobs also had many dud products on his resume prior to the Mac, iPhone and iPod victories. Another successful failure, Albert Einstein, a great genius in science and life, is noted as having said, "Failure is success in progress." The key to failure is in not giving up. Innovator and inventor Thomas Edison said, "Many of life's failures are people who did not realize how close they were to success when they gave up."

Why is it that people quit after they fail? I believe the answer is quite simple. Failure hurts. Failure tries to convince us that we are not good enough, not smart enough, and not tenacious enough to succeed. Failure rocks us at our very core. It's the voice in our head that says, "See, I told you so." It's every bully we came across when we were growing up, beating us down mentally. It's every bad boss, unfriendly coworker and unsupportive family member we have had in our lives. But we need to look beyond all the bad that failure sends in our direction. We need to focus on what happens beyond failure. As humans, we are sometimes short-sighted. We have a challenge moving beyond the pain of now, and seeing the pleasure of tomorrow.

The best outcome we get from failure is that we get a lesson. We get a story. We gain knowledge, strength and power to move on. In some cases, failure should motivate us to work harder on a project. In some cases, failure teaches us the project we are working on is not worth continuing. But in every case, failure teaches us a lesson.

Failure, similar to success has a specific set of characteristics. There is generally a reason why people fail. Pertaining to business, here are the reasons why people fail.

Everything to everybody, equals nothing for me.

Being a jack of all trades will quickly put you in the loss column. When I started my speaking career I hired a speaking coach, Jane Atkinson. Jane, owner of Speaker Launcher, taught me on day one to "pick a lane." She helped me realize quickly that if the world was my market and marketed my business to the world at large, I would be in big trouble. And she was right. We all need to narrow our focus. I started to develop a marketing plan that incorporated my strengths in sales and marketing, and I created a message that would specifically reach that market. The market you will be providing products or services to wants an expert. Imagine going to your dentist and seeing a sign at the check-in desk that says "Pizza delivery, shoe shine and pet sitting available." How would that make you feel? Not good. If you are like me, you want someone that has made an investment in his career. Pick your lane, dedicate yourself to your choice, learn everything you can and work hard to be successful. Being a Jack of all trades will not earn my business.

Don't have time? You are likely to fail unless you make time.

Being successful requires time. Lots of it. I always joke with my friends that are in the "real world" and have real jobs. I tell them there is no better feeling than working all day in my pajamas. Being self-employed is great because I also get to pick which 18 hours a day I get to work my business. In order for success to be your result, you have got to spend time going after it. Success is a full-time job. If you are starting a business and are already working a full-time job, I strongly urge you to develop a business plan consisting of your plan of action. You'll need to eliminate everything in your life (maybe only temporarily) considered a time suck. Start by turning off the television. According to a recent Nielsen study, the average American spends over 30 hours a week watching television. In 2012 I cut the cable and went cold turkey from television watching. I've regained control of my "free time" and have been able to focus my efforts of building my business. In addition, I have been able to find more balance in my life as well. Prepare yourself to make time for success. It will require lots of time.

Small thinking equals small results.

Les Brown, motivational speaker, author and business resource, said, "Shoot for the moon, even if you miss, you will land among the stars." Think big, why not? You should have some lofty yet realistic goals. Strive to be the best you can be. Never set a goal to come in second place. Go for the gold and think with your heart. Most people fail because they set goals that are too small and end up not being able to survive.

In 2014, I submitted a blog to Arianna Huffington, founder of The Huffington Post. I never actually considered she would read my e-mail or my post, but hoping she would, I was delighted when she responded to my e-mail directly. I was even happier that she liked my blog and added it to her publication. I am proud to say that I am now a regular contributor to Huffington Post. Think big, it may just pay off.

Dr. David J. Schwartz penned *The Magic of Thinking Big*. In the book he writes about improving your job, marriage and family life through thinking and behaving in ways to help you develop the habits of success. Dr. Schwartz describes in detail the importance of positive thinking, believing in yourself, and developing habits of a leader. He also talks about the fact that anyone can achieve success because anyone can think like a winner. You do not need to be highly educated, smarter or more qualified to be successful. "Success is determined not so much by the size of one's brain as it is by the size of one's thinking."

Failure to take responsibility.

The blame game is very easy to play. People are quick to shift responsibility, make excuses and ignore the fact that they are in charge of themselves. Character plays a huge role in determining success and one way to fail is to blame someone else for setbacks and problems.

As owner of an entertainment company for over twenty years I have watched many extremely talented disc jockeys fail in business because they would blame anyone but themselves for issues relating to the business. We have a simple rule, you must call your client at least one week in advance prior to event date in order to go over event details and to introduce yourself to the client. You would think that a rule like this would be easy to follow. Think again. I would have acts call a day or two prior to event day asking me questions about the party. My question in return is always the same, "When you spoke to the client earlier in the week, what did they tell you?" Most would say, "I tried to reach the client and they never called me back." It is so very frustrating when these incredibly talented people do not take responsibility for themselves.

If you can train yourself to take excuses out of your life, you will be making a huge dent in the causes for failure. The next time you feel like blaming someone else for your situation, stop and think about the energy you are about to expend on making the excuse, and use that same energy and develop a solution for the problem.

Success is up to you. No one is responsible for the outcome other than you, and the sooner you realize it, the faster you will become responsible for yourself and on your way to success.

Failure to have a system.

I dedicate an entire chapter of this book to systems. Systems are required in order to help you be successful. Lack of systems in your business will set you up for failure. My Nice Guy system is simple and consists of three basic steps. Invest. Inspire. Execute. What's great is that there is not just one correct system. Pick and choose from thousands or create a system of your own and stick to it. People that fail in business usually are not following a system, or if they have a system in place they are not consistent about using it. Again, I dedicate another chapter in this book to consistency as a qualifier for success.

I would suggest that if you are busy, and who isn't these days, you adopt a system that includes time management. I personally feel as though the best systems that have been developed are simple to use, have a basis in automation (use it as a tool, not a crutch), and set up a routine that you can follow daily.

Planning is the most important aspect to avoid the pitfalls to failure. The great inventor, politician and historical figure Ben Franklin is credited with saying, "If you fail to plan, you are planning to fail." Planning can be as simple as a set of goals written down on a napkin or as intricate as an entire business plan presented to a venture capitalist. The process should be ready, aim, fire. It should not be ready, fire, aim.

Action Items

1. Write down 3 impressive failures that you have gone through professionally and what lessons you have learned from them.

2. List 5 ways that a positive attitude can help you avoid failure, or if you do fail, how a positive attitude can get you back on track from your failure.

3. The next time you find you are about to make an excuse for failing at something, STOP! It's easy to make an excuse. Take responsibility, work harder at improving and stay positive. Excuses will not help you succeed. Action will.

CHAPTER 13

MISTAKES NICE GUYS NEED TO AVOID

A man must be big enough to admit his mistakes, smart enough to profit from them, and strong enough to correct them.

~John C. Maxwell

While speaking to groups on the topic of finishing first, I spend a lot of time talking about the reasons why building a positive experience is a big part of building exceptional customer service. A part of building a positive experience is understanding the mistakes that you need to avoid when dealing with any prospect or current client. Over the years, most of the jobs I have had put me on the frontline, selling and dealing directly with customers.

I noticed a pattern started to develop when I would not make a sale or make a customer completely happy. It wasn't until years later when I owned my own business that I recognized that by making these mistakes, even one of them, I had a high likelihood of either losing a sale or losing a customer. When you are newly self-employed, a lost sale can mean the difference between staying in business and going out of business. Even established customers that I had a good relationship with could be lost if the mistake was key enough. To help me avoid making these mistakes I wrote them down, studied them, adjusted them, tweaked them and made a master plan to do everything in my power to NOT have these mistakes creep into my behavior.

As I developed a program to teach others about how to build better relationships with customers, I also studied their behavior to verify that making these five mistakes in the selling cycle or in the process of delivering customer service was not specific to me. Meaning, these same mistakes, if made by someone else, would also result in the same outcome of a lost sale or unhappy customer.

Why is it that some people in sales and customer service positions succeed while others have challenges on a daily basis that they can't seem to figure out? Why is it that you can take someone who does quite well selling real estate, put them in a position selling any other product or service, and they will still succeed? Some might say, "That guy is a born salesman!" Or they might say, "He's just a good people person." Maybe those two things are true. Or maybe, just maybe, these same success stories have done enough things *wrong*, enough times, to figure out what it is that they are doing RIGHT.

One thing for sure, over the last 25 years, I've made every mistake in the book, and it's a long book. Given enough time, I would be happy to list the one thousand and thirty-seven mistakes that have created setbacks, roadblocks, failures and lost opportunities for me and for those I have studied. Keep in mind, as you review these mistakes, they apply to more than just business. These are great life lessons too. I think it's important to note that as you begin to review the list, if you are guilty of committing one or all of the mistakes, all is not completely lost. You have a shot at redemption; it's as simple as that. But you will need to STOP making the mistake.

Let me make one GUARANTEE before I lay it out. If you fail to make a change in your behavior, I guarantee you that you are taking the long path to success. To put yourself on the short track to success in business and in life, make these changes quickly, without hesitation and continue to review your progress. Daily.

Mistake #1 Failure to Listen

Sounds pretty simple right? Common sense? Why on earth would people not listen to their prospect or their customer?

For the life of me, this one is so simple, I cannot figure out why anyone in a position of sales or service would not listen. As I write this I am sitting in my hotel room. I noticed upon entering the room, the glassware was dirty. I called down to the front desk and asked for a few new glasses. Within 5 minutes, Jane, from housekeeping, knocked on the door. As I opened the door to her smiling face, she proudly, but apologetically, was holding an ice bucket in her hand.

I thanked her for her quick response but told her that I had requested new glasses and not an ice bucket. Within 30 seconds I was having a conversation with Jane about her conversation with the front desk and how they told her to bring me a clean ice bucket. This national hotel chain was not about to lose my travel business because they gave me an ice bucket instead of glasses, but it would have made me feel as though my words were important had the front desk just LISTENED to what I had asked for.

Let me make it as clear as day for you. You MUST listen to what people are telling you. Books have been written on the subject of good listening skills. There is a wonderful philosophy called the Fish Philosophy developed by John Christensen. Mr. Christensen created this philosophy in 1998 and since the launch of this ideology many companies and schools have adopted his program. One of the keys to his program is being present and being in the moment. An ongoing practice of mindfulness. This generally means being present and listening while you're at work (and home) in both your body *and* your mind, and making that extra effort to avoid wandering off into the world of daydreams. It also means being there for coworkers, colleagues, friends and family and simply paying attention to what you're doing.

Mistake #2 Over Promise and Underdeliver

Rhonda, who managed a retail business that sold yoga mats, had a morning meeting with a local supplier of yoga mats, a product she was looking for. Everything seemed to be going along perfectly well. They had the yoga mat color and quantity she was looking for in stock. The delivery time seemed to be within the time frame she required, 30 days. The payment terms were great, net 60 days. All she needed now was a proposal from the salesperson she had just had a meeting with. At the end of the meeting, the salesperson said, "Thanks, Rhonda, I will have this proposal over to you in a couple hours. I'm heading back to my office now."

All was good with the world. Rhonda could actually see her company stocking the shelves with yoga mats. And she was so excited because they finally had the color that her boss wanted. After heading out to lunch Rhonda checked her e-mail from her iPhone. No proposal. She made a quick call over to her supplier rep, but he was out to lunch. She left him a message and fired off a quick text. "Looking for proposal. When should I expect to see it?" He replied quickly, "You'll have it by close of business." She was disappointed since it wasn't exactly what she had been promised, but things were ok. She could deal with it. Close of business came and still no proposal. A call in the morning to her sales rep, and she discovered the color was on backorder but would be available to ship to her company prior to her deadline with her customer. She also found out her company would have to pay hefty deposit. Rhonda's salesperson said he would do her a "favor" and have a portion of the deposit waived. The entire experience left a bad flavor in Rhonda's mouth. But she moved forward with the sale anyway. Next time she will look for another supplier.

The above scenario is not uncommon. Sales people often make the costly mistake of over promising. When presented with an opportunity to close a deal, sales people can get so excited they may over promise but then under deliver. We have all experienced the feeling of being on the short end of that stick; and it's disappointing. "We want to please others and make them happy. Sometimes clouded, we tell them what we think they want to hear."

Let's take the above scene and do our best to fix it. Rhonda finishes up the morning meeting and she gets a call about 30 minutes later. It's her salesperson on the line. "Rhonda, I am putting the proposal together right now. I've checked with my manufacturing plant and discovered that we just had a huge order for yoga mats in your color late last week. We have a couple of solutions, can you let me know if either one will work for you? I can ship another color to you tomorrow, if the color isn't critical, or we can wait until the color you want is in stock, which is still well in advance of your needed date. I am confident I can have the deposit waived since you are one of my VIP clients. I really appreciate your business, Rhonda." He gets the order, and Rhonda feels good about how her order was handled.

Part of human nature is the desire to want to please others and make them happy. Sometimes clouded, we tell them what we think they want to hear. It is only ok if we are able to deliver what we are promising and come through for them 100% of the time. Resist the urge to please your client with words alone. Over promising and under delivering is a formula for problems and losing customers.

In the late summer of 2009, I took a business trip with the owners of Washington Talent Agency to Las Vegas. The trip was always a combination of business and pleasure. The two owners of the agency, Chuck Kahanov and Robert Sherman, treated many of the agency acts to a fun few days. We would stay at great hotels, have amazing meals, and although we would be kicking back and enjoying life for a few days, we actually accomplished some business too. On this particular trip while sitting at dinner, we discussed the plans for the next day over a glass of cabernet and amazing steak. We heard about this company called Zappos that was so good at providing customer service, delivering on promises and creating an extremely positive work culture, that they ran tours of their corporate headquarters located in Las Vegas.

Always wanting to understand why and how things worked (especially when they worked well), I was excited to find out that they had openings for a tour the very next day. As we toured the "floor" we learned that the founder of Zappos, Tony Hsieh, was extreme in his capacity to deliver award-winning service. Mr. Hsieh wrote a book called *Delivering Happiness* that discusses, among many other things, the importance of setting very high expectations and making sure to exceed those expectations. If you have not heard of the Zappos story or ever wanted to experience how effective a positive culture is on the bottom line, visit them or read about the climb of this billion dollar online retailer. You will be amazed.

Mistake #3 Poor Response Time and Follow-Up

We are bombarded on a daily basis by information. Many of us spend the majority of our day in front of a computer, tablet, iPad, iPhone, Blackberry or other piece of hardware. The information overload age we are currently in makes it challenging for us to filter out all the junk and determine what is the good stuff. Good stuff is defined as any e-mail, call, text or piece of information that has a personal connection to us and needs our attention now.

I recently had the opportunity to hire a musician for an event. I left a message for the musician's agent to request the date. Several days had gone by and I did not receive a call back. I followed up again. Still no return call. On my third attempt to reach the agent, they picked up, but I was met with a barrage of excuses for no follow-up. "Sorry, I didn't recognize the phone number or your name, I was going to call back, but I thought you might be closed for the holiday. It was a very busy weekend and I hadn't gotten around to returning the call yet." These excuses are the reason I selected another musician.

I had no reason to believe they would take care of me or my client or deliver on event day solely based on my attempt to contact them.

When faced with a situation of following up with a potential customer, it is critical that you do it quickly. Even if you call back to say "I just got your message, I want to talk to you, can we schedule a brief phone call? Your call is important, and I didn't want to delay in getting back to you." Response time via computer should be even quicker. I was recently told by someone they respond to their business e-mails within 24 hours. I don't like the 24 hour "rule." I feel if you are taking 24 hours to respond to an e-mail, your client today will be someone else's tomorrow.

What it comes down to is this. When the phone rings, when a text message is received, when you get an e-mail, or when any situation arises that requires follow-up, it is critical that you follow-up in a timely manner. Failure to do so will result in lost clients, lost referrals and lost relationships. Take responsibility for following up as if your business depends on it, because it does.

Mistake #4 Failure to Have a System

Systems are designed for success, just like we discussed earlier about the McDonald's system. But systems do not need to be huge or even franchised in order to be successful. My step-dad Marty is in his late eighties. Marty, now retired for nearly 20 years sat down with me to discuss how systems and business in general has changed since he started working in the 1940s. I was surprised to find that although technology has changed the way we sell and conduct business since the 1940s, the need and use of systems was popular back then as well.

Marty began his career as a door-to-door encyclopedia salesman. He had to knock on 100 doors, in order to get 5 appointments. Five appointments with the decision maker got him 2 sales. It was easy for him to figure out how many times he needed to knock on doors in order to make his ten sale quota. Five hundred knocks. That's a system as well.

Obviously, times have changed and knocking on doors is seemingly archaic. We now have technology to our advantage. With the aid of analytics, everything can be, and is, measured. Hits on our website, page views, time spent on each page and a variety of statistics help us determine our goals based upon web traffic. There are contact management programs and apps designed to help keep things organized

However, don't get caught in the trap of "paralysis through analysis." Because there are so many options and so many systems, many people can't decide which the best is for them to use, the easiest to use, and the most productive to use. They end up not using any system for fear of not selecting correctly.

I developed a system early on in my career with a specific agenda. Keep it simple. The system that I put in place in 1991 as a foundation for my business practice remains the same now as it was in 1991.

1. Tell the truth

2. Return my phone calls

3. Be a nice guy

Since creating *Nice Guys Finish First* I have added 3 more to my system:

1. Invest

2. Inspire

3. Execute

When in doubt, and unsure of what system to go to, use the resources you have to help you find a system that will work for you. If you work for a large organization, I can almost guarantee they have a system in place to generate and track leads, manage your time, develop business and manage contacts and goals. If you need help to determine the best system for you, consider speaking to someone who has been doing what you do but is more experienced and ok with lending a helping hand. In general, I have found people very willing to assist. I would also encourage you to continue reading about my system. Whatever system you determine is best for you, I suggest that you own it, and do not stray from the agenda it lays out.

Mistake #5 Failure to Care

The grandaddy of them all. If you don't care about your customer and the results, you are going to have trouble convincing others to buy your products or services. You must care about your customers and prospects. If you run a department filled with script readers, order takers or technology specialists, you MUST teach them how to be human as well. Being human is not an option, it's a necessity. People like dealing with other people, not emotionless machines. Machines do not care and have no emotion. Think about how you feel when you are stuck on an automated call and can't reach a person. People who do not express emotion are no better than machines.

A couple of years ago I was out of town and rented a motorcycle. When I parked the bike overnight, the travel bags were stolen off the motorcycle from the hotel's garage. When I called the insurance company representative, I was "greeted" by a customer service rep that treated me more like a number than a person at that moment.

I couldn't determine which was worse—the feeling of invasion since my motorcycle had been vandalized or the process of trying to claim the theft with the insurance company. A short lesson in empathy would have gone a long way for that representative, and I would have felt more at ease and less violated had I reached someone whom I thought cared about my situation rather than the insurance company's bottom line.

If it sounds like you are reading a script when talking to your customer on the phone, the recipient of said script can tell that you are reading from a script. I understand that many sales and service departments must have a script in order to measure results, but please make sure you care about your customer. You may want to practice with a friend. Get feedback about how you sound, how you can improve, and how your approach made them feel. If you give your customer a reason to move to your competition, they will.

I had the opportunity to connect with Jeremy Watkin, a blogger, and 12 plus year customer service veteran, who writes on the subject of caring about your customers. Jeremy and fellow blogger Jenny Dempsey offer a weekly YouTube podcast called the "Coffee and Customer Service Hangout." In the hangout they talk about the issues and trends in customer service, industry hot topics and their Communicate Better blog.

I shared with Jeremy my 5 Biggest Mistakes, but we spoke mostly on this last mistake—the lack of caring. Jeremy is passionate when he talks about caring. He said, "Caring customer service must permeate the entire organization, inside and out and from top to bottom." Caring means making personal emotional connections. It means appreciating your customers even before they are customers. In addition, it means taking ownership of each problem that surfaces and not relinquishing ownership until the problem is solved. Finally Jeremy adds, "Never forget at the core of customer service is the act of serving people. Put these characteristics to work when you serve others and you will show the people in your life that you care."

Action Items

1. Of the 5 biggest mistakes above, which mistake do you think you make the most and why? What are you going to do to avoid making this mistake?

2. List 2 other mistakes that you "see" in your world and write down your plan to avoid these mistakes as well.

3. Describe a system in place that you use on a regular basis to help keep you focused on good habits in business.

CHAPTER 14

NICE GUYS MANAGE A BETTER LIFE

You only live once, but if you do it right, once is enough.

~Mae West

There is a huge laundry list of things that we could use help managing in our lives. I wish I was smart enough as a young adult to follow the advice given to me by many successful people including those that were closest to me and those that I trusted.

As I got into my professional world, I was given advice on the importance of managing my life better. It wasn't like I was doing a bad job at running my life, but there were many wise people that lived great lives before me, just like there are many others that have gone before you; so why not learn from their mistakes? My father always talked to me about the concepts found in books by Napoleon Hill, Dale Carnegie, Zig Ziglar, Steven Covey and many other experts in the field of self-help and people management. Many of my managers, coworkers, partners and friends have been avid readers, and because I heeded their advice, I too fell in love with reading and learning about improving myself.

For me, managing my life was about controlling the things that oftentimes would get out of control. So I developed a list of the things that I felt like I needed the most help with, and as this list revealed itself to me, I thought about the ways in which I would be able to manage them as well.

Patience

Like a rubber band that gets stretched to its limit, patience expands when put into practice. But no matter how much practice we get with patience, we could all use a bit more of it in our lives. The patience we have will often get tested. Coworkers, customers, family members and especially the guy standing in line in front of you at Starbucks trying to order his triple venti half-sweet nonfat caramel macchiato will test your patience. As you feel your blood pressure start to rise when pushed to your limit, do your best to take a breath. Try to relax and realize that it is temporary, and life will return to normal any moment. Personally, I defeat escalating blood pressure and stretched patience by laughing it off. I try to keep in mind that whomever is testing my patience level is not actually doing it on purpose. A customer that doesn't understand the answer to my question, the coworker that needs that e-mail answered now, your kid who lost his cell phone again and that guy at Starbucks ordering his specialty coffee—they all have problems that need resolution, and they are not doing anything to you. Be a part of the solution instead of escalating the problem with patience stretched thin.

Management Techniques

1. Try to determine whatthe triggers are for your impatience.

2. Start to see the big picture instead of focusing on the now.

3. Have a positive outlook and a positive attitude about life.

4. Don't act on impulse, give yourself a moment to give your best response.

5. Consider the source, and act accordingly if the situation is outside of your control.

Time

We all have the same 24 hours a day in which to work our plan, both professionally and personally. And time management is something everyone can use more of. Look at it this way, if you were given 28 hours in a day, you would push the limits of 28 hours each and every day. It's not like you have ever seen a productive adult standing around saying, "I am all done with my to-do list today, so I am just gonna hang out until I'm given my 24 hours tomorrow." By nature, human beings push the limits. We try to cram in as many appointments, phone calls, e-mails, Tweets, carpool rides and homework sessions with our kids as possible. Here are a couple of solutions that may work for you. First, cut the cable. Television is the biggest time suck of all. Become a reader and feed your brain with good stuff. A quick read like Ken Blanchard's *One Minute Manager* is a great start. No time for reading? Listen to it on audio while driving to an appointment. We are put on this earth for a finite period of time. Do not waste the time you are given on brainless activities. Cut the cable, pick up a book, hug your kid, and be more productive with your time.

Management techniques

1. Write down your schedule and allow it to guide you through your day.

2. Plan out your day before it gets out of control.

3. Learn to say "No" to tasks or distractions if they are outside of your scope.

4. Delegate to others especially if others are better qualified to handle the task.

5. Don't sweat the details. Sometimes small stuff is just that, small stuff.

<u>Money</u>

In our society, the need for money is not something we should be ashamed of or that we should be fearful of talking about it. By definition, money greases our economy. And no matter our position on the subject of money (love it, hate it, never have enough of it), we cannot dispute that we need it to acquire the stuff that is essential in our lives. Whether it's sending our kids to college, helping with an ailing parent's medical bills, saving it for a much needed vacation or just going out for a pizza, the lack of money is the cause of many problems we encounter. Some of us need help making more money and some need a lesson in what to do with it once we get it. And we love to count other people's money. We can't quite understand how people that make a lot of money manage to blow it all, while we fail to realize there are people that make less than us that are saying the same thing about us.

One common theme is that we all need help managing it. Here are a couple of common rules that you need to follow in order to manage your money.

Rule 1: Pay yourself first - Regardless of how much you pay yourself, write a check to yourself every month. Make it easy and have it on auto-withdraw. In a couple of months you will not miss the money. That account has one purpose and one direction, and that is for depositing fund ONLY.

Rule 2: Find a professional and come up with a plan for your future. The excuse, "I have no money, so why do I need a professional to help me manage it?" is not valid. You will never have any money unless you either enlist a professional to help you or you figure out a way to change the habits that got you broke to begin with.

Rule 3: Budget your funds in today's dollars. Be realistic about what you spend your money on and where your money is going. An easy way to do this is to track for 30 days every penny you spend. You will be amazed at exactly where you can cut back when you realize you spend $140 on lunch, $80 on coffee, and $150 on your cable bill (see time management above).

Management techniques

1. Follow a monthly budget. The easiest way to manage money is to control it on a monthly schedule.

2. Contribute to a regular savings plan or a retirement plan.

3. Be a wise consumer and do not spend money without doing research, especially on the large purchases.

4. Set financial goals and monitor the goals on a regular basis to see

how you are doing.

5. Educate yourself as to the best methods to manage your finances. You care about your finances more than anyone else, so it's your job to read, learn and plan for your future.

Relationships

We are constantly learning from others. As we grow more relationships, we develop of sense of perspective and diversity. Although we want relationships to be easy, good relationships require effort, and rightfully so, because we can learn an awful lot from others, so they are worth the investment. Take time to nurture new relationships and stay connected to established relationships.

The best piece of advice I can offer about relationships is *communicate*. Communicate often, with honest, open, helpful words. For family and friends, tell them you love them, care about them and that you appreciate them in your life. For clients, coworkers and others in your life, tell them you love them, care about them and appreciate them in your life. Are you catching a common theme?

Be connected, be personal and most of all, be yourself. Never feel like you have to prove a point or be right all the time; and never be afraid to say "I'm sorry" or "I was wrong." You will not reach your goals in life alone. The people you have relationships with are going to be a part of Team You, just like you are a part of Team Them.

Follow the Golden Rule and treat them with love and respect and they will return the favor. It is unlikely that you will ever love or be loved too much, that you will ever be too nice or that you will ever be too helpful; give each of these a try, I promise the results will be amazing.

Management techniques

1. Communicate and listen to those you have relationships with. It is less important to be right and more important to listen.

2. Resolve conflicts as they happen. Do not hang on to problems or let them accumulate. The expression, "Never go to bed angry" is important. Do your best to work out conflicts quickly.

3. Understand that change is the only thing that is constant. People, personalities and situations in life change. Allow change to be a part of your relationships.

4. Trust each other and understand that people you are involved with personally and professionally need to both work toward a common goal.

5. Perspective in a relationship will allow you to understand the person you are involved with. Try to see things from their perspective and have a greater understanding of what they are trying to achieve.

Freedom

We all strive to be independent. Freedom thrust upon someone who has always been dependent upon others provides challenges of its own. For example, giving a young adult complete freedom to make their own decisions when they first go to college can result in huge challenges if we do not help them manage their freedom. When a lifetime employee strikes out on his own as a self-employed business owner a sure fire way for failure is to get no help from others managing your new found freedom. Freedom to make your own decisions, to be your own boss and to lead your own way is an awesome responsibility and full of amazing potential.

Your best bet for finding your proper path is to see what others have done before you. If you are new to self-employment for example, find someone successful that has done what you do for a longer period of time and ask them for help. You will be amazed how helpful people are and how much information they are willing to provide. When I first got involved with professional speaking and coaching, I got online and started contacting other speakers, authors and coaches. Every single person I approached provided practical, everyday, essential advice on getting started.

Mastermind groups are another great way to help manage freedom. I first read about mastermind groups decades ago when I read a book by Napolean Hill called *Think and Grow Rich*. Defined - a small group that you meet with for the purpose of reinforcing growth and success while offering support to one another. Freedom allows you to make choices and be in control of your own destiny, but it is critical to have help managing your freedom, or you will find yourself under of "rule" of someone else if you manage your freedom improperly. The best part about freedom is that you are free to walk where your heart leads you. And that is an incredible feeling.

Management techniques

1. Learn from others and take action based upon their experiences.

2. Get moving now. The best way to achieve freedom in your life is through action.

3. Don't be so critical of yourself. Not everyone is perfect, and neither are you, but that's ok. Don't let your own negative self-talk hold you back from being free.

4. Don't be afraid to fail. Show me a successful person, and I will

show you someone that has failed many times before achieving success.

5. Don't let fear hold you back. Fear will be your worst enemy as you approach freedom. Instead of letting fear hold you back, use it as your motivation to move closer to your goals.

As you approach each of these areas, it is up to you to tailor your management techniques to help you gain control of each of the areas. Don't look at the list as an overwhelming set of problems in need of resolution. My dad used to tell me problems are like elephants. If we were to eat the elephant, we would not just gulp it down. The best way to eat an elephant is one slice at a time. Action is the best remedy to managing any of the areas above. Take a slice from one of the sections and begin to work on it today. Prioritize. Which section challenges you most? Don't save that one for last, begin to slice it up and resolve it now. If managing finances is your biggest hurdle, know that you are among good company. Start by putting $100 in an envelope. There is nothing complicated about putting money away. Most people simply don't do it.

I can promise you that by gaining control and managing each of the above areas, goals that you have set for yourself will begin to be achieved. As you practice each technique, you will get better at them. Money will start to go into savings, your schedule will not control you, you will develop better, more meaningful relationships, people will be amazed by your level of patience and all the freedom that you could ever dream of will be yours to enjoy.

Action Items

1. What areas of your life need better management? Prioritize the 5 areas above from 1 to 5. If you have other areas of your life in need of management, add them to your list as well.

2. List the management techniques from above in each of the areas that you need to do a better job at establishing or utilizing. For example, in the money management area above, if you do not have a budget in place, list "need a budget" as an item.

3. Take action now on improving these areas of your life. The management techniques above are just the beginning. Work hard at forming new, positive habits to manage your life.

CHAPTER 15

NICE GUYS LESSONS ABOUT LIFE AND BUSINESS

Two roads diverged in a wood, and I, I took the one
less traveled by, and that has made all the difference.

~Robert Frost

Goals are funny things. They are the big picture plans we put together when we come up with a crazy idea like writing a book. Our goals are the things that we shoot for like starting a new career or buying a new home. Goals are the target in the distant future that will lead us to our dreams.

Along the path from inception to completion, reality sets in, and our plans get adjusted, sidetracked, bumped, stepped on, and pushed around. By the time we take a moment to turn around and see the path we took to get here, we realize it wasn't at all a straight path to our goals. As I turn around and look at the past several months of writing, and the interpretation of exactly what happened to me over the last half century since I entered this world, nothing that I ever accomplished was a straight path. It was all a mess.

Life can be a crooked mess of paths that lead us to our goals that eventually lead us to our dreams. I guess the word mess is not the best choice of words since it implies disarray and a lack of order. Just the opposite, however, applies to my goals, as I hope it applies to yours as well. Yes, I must admit sometimes I have no idea what I am doing on this path, and I get scared as hell thinking I will get hopelessly lost. But I have always kept my eye on my goals.

We have all heard the expression countless times, "It's not the destination, it's the journey." And while I agree that we should all spend a bit more time loving the present moment and cherishing the memories we are creating right here and now, oftentimes I have put my blinders on and focused only on my dreams because the journey gets really tough along the way. Sometimes life isn't fair, and if you are reading this book, I am confident you have also experienced the sting of unfairness, the frustration of "Why did that just happen to me?" and disbelief of "I can't believe that just happened. That's not fair."

Experience, acquired knowledge and the time tested school of hard knocks in my personal and professional relationships has led me to better understand many things I wish I would had known earlier in my life. As you read the list below, take a moment and consider how these things fit into your world also. Don't read the list as my list, read the list as it would apply to your relationships, your business, your clients and your world. Take another moment after reading the list and write down anything you would add to this list as well.

Had I known back in 1977 when I first entered the work world as a kid or even in 1986 when I graduated from college, what I know now, I would have worked harder at building relationships, cherished the brief moments of the many victories I have experienced and dismissed the pain faster of the losses I endured.

1. Not everyone is a good customer for you.

2. Everything can be overcome through action.

3. Sometimes things are just beyond our control, and that's ok.

4. You are in charge of your behavior.

5. As surprising as it is to me, not everyone is going to like me.

6. Customer service rule one - deliver on every promise. Rule two - see rule one.

7. Common sense is not so common.

8. Nothing great was ever achieved by doing nothing great.

9. It's better to have a happy client.

10. Saying "NO" is not always a bad thing.

11. Saying "YES" is not always a good thing.

12. Clients are sometimes unrealistic about their expectations and it's ok to gently tell them.

13. Nothing says thank you better than a handwritten thank you note.

14. The customer is ALWAYS right, even when they aren't right. (It's your job to figure out how to make them right.)

15. Saying I'm sorry is the first step in dealing with an unhappy client. Get good at it.

16. Being an expert in something doesn't mean telling everything you know, every time.

17. The best road to take is not always the one most traveled.

18. Laughing at yourself is best for a healthy self-esteem

19. Just because you know your client's budget doesn't mean you have to spend it all.

20. When you are e-mailed questions from a client, it's a good idea to answer every question. Not just the ones important to you.

21. Thinking outside the box doesn't pay the bills immediately, so get a job until your inside the box ideas don't fit inside the box anymore.

22. Being 15 minutes late is not on time.

23. You are your own worst critic already. Learn to be your biggest encourager as well.

24. Alarm clocks are not my friend, so I have learned to not use them.

25. Listening is much better than talking. When in doubt, shut up.

26. Be brain engaged before putting your mouth in gear.

27. There are many instances when signing "XOXO" on your signature line is ok.

28. Never underestimate the power of one, especially if that one is you.

29. Don't discount the power of a good hug.

30. Smiles are extremely contagious. Go ahead, give it a try.

31. Conference calls and meetings should be used as a last resort.

32. Attitude is everything.

33. Never have a disagreement via text, e-mail or social media.

34. Bookstores have these things called books in them with tons of useful information.

35. Know a good idea when you steal it. And give proper credit.

36. Catching someone doing something right will build a strong connection for you.

37. Stopping to smell the roses is more than just an expression.

38. I'll call you right back is not just an expression.

39. When someone compliments you on a job well done, be humble.

40. Never quit, even when you fail, make adjustments and keep moving.

41. Without support, reaching your goals will be impossible. Accept help.

42. Fear is normal, but don't let it hold you back.

43. Nobody is watching, it's ok to dance a little when you succeed.

44. Nobody is watching, it's ok to cry when you hit a bump in the road.

45. Fair is a place with Ferris wheels and fried dough. Sometimes life isn't fair.

46. If given the choice between reliable and skillful, choose reliable. You can train skill.

47. Be yourself and no one else. There is no better you than you.

48. Live each and every day with love in your heart.

49. Live with purpose, be the best you can be.

50. Nice guys finish first.

So, why exactly do nice guys finish first, and why is it that I set out to try and spread this message? I have a belief, as many others do, that people are basically good. We all stumble every once and again, but given an opportunity to choose between right and wrong, the vast majority of people will pick right over wrong. I would also argue that most people are nice, and we just need to get some help trying to figure out what the right thing to do is and exactly how to do it.

There is no complete manual on how to live life, or if there is something like a manual, it is handed to us when we are about get on a real bumpy ride, written in a very tiny font, and we can't hold on to it or focus on the words as we are on the journey.

All of us are holding in our hands our book (life). Each and every day you are writing your lessons down in the form of memories. It would be a great idea to write down some of the lessons you are learning. It may not be because you have a goal of writing a book, but instead, because you are keeping a life journal. It may be that only you will read your journal. Or you might possibly share it with your children if you decide you want to share your legacy with others.

Whatever the case, I encourage you to learn from your lessons and take away anything positive, leaving the negative behind. Life is too short to hate, too short to be bitter, too short to hold a grudge and definitely too short to miss an opportunity to be happy and love.

Seek out adventure in your life. Adventure doesn't mean you have to go on a jungle safari, or change jobs every year or jump out of an airplane. Adventure might simply mean doing all the things that make you happy and none of the things that make you unhappy. If you are not fulfilled with where you are in life, do an assessment of where you are and take action. If you are not happy or satisfied with your job, find a new one or figure out how to make yourself happy in your current position. If you are personally in a bad place, find support in friends, family or professional help and determine what it is that is making your life challenging and then make a change.

Indecision and inactivity are usually caused by fear. It's ok to have fear, but it is not ok to let fear paralyze you. Action is the enemy to fear. Work hard at looking past the fear. Face the truth that you have fear but visualize yourself on the other side of it. Be a part of the solution, not the problem.

Challenge yourself to focus on your goals. The idea of change conjures feelings of the unknown. Instead of focusing your thoughts on the unknown, focus on your dreams. Visualize the rewards success will bring you. Fear of failure holds us all back at some point. When we go through it, failure bruises our self-esteem, causes regret and deflates our ego. However, moving beyond failure, the rewards can be awesome. Put yourself in gear and make life happen.

Life can be like a merry-go-round, the same view, predictable and serene. Or life can be like a roller coaster with twists and turns, loops and huge falls and thrills galore. Have you ever wondered why the merry-go-round is two tickets and the roller coast is twelve tickets? Because it's worth it. Make your life worth it.

And don't forget, nice guys (and girls) finish first.

CPSIA information can be obtained
at www.ICGtesting.com
Printed in the USA
FFOW01n2333171016
28558FF